The Consent Primer

Foundations for Everyday Life

by The Consent Academy

Sar Surmick, Rachel Drake, Lara-Ashley Monroe, Kelley O'Hanlon, & Leah Hirsch

First Edition

ISBN-13: 978-1-7338203-0-1
ISBN-10: 1-7338203-0-2

Cover design by: Robin Harper 2019

This book is dedicated to all the consent explorers, advocates, warriors, experts, scholars, educators, and thinkers that came before. We also acknowledge the often thankless work done by those placed in non-consensual spaces and interactions who strove to understand what was happening to them, to overcome the harm done, and to speak out. If we have seen further, and created something significant, it is because we have been lifted up by those that came before.

Special thanks to:

Our friends and families who have put up with both the untold hours of work that went into this text and our constant musings, exploration, and questions around consent.

The Pan Eros Foundation for all of its support.

The Consent Academy Volunteers: past, present, and future. There is no way to adequately thank you for the thousands of hours you've already dedicated to this complex and critical topic. Your dedication, support, and insight have made this work possible.

Everyone who has come to our workshops, consult groups, brainstorming sessions, retreats, and meetings. We wouldn't have made it this far without you.

Our beta-readers who caught many of our mistakes and made this work so much better.

And you dedicated reader, for sharing our first book.

Contents

Introduction

Consent is Essential.

Consent is for Everyone.

And Consent is complicated!

What is consent? This is the first and probably most relevant question. To give a formal definition: Consent is a voluntary agreement, made without coercion, between persons with decision-making capacity, knowledge, understanding, and autonomy. The use of consent allows a person to affirm or deny any request or interaction.

So, what does that mean?

At its most basic, consent allows us to say yes or no to something. As such, it covers all forms of interactions. Anything you do with another person can involve some form of consent. While many people only think of consent as something that happens around sex or sexual interactions, we want you to think of it as something that happens constantly, every day, in a hundred different ways.

Consent is something you do because you want to. No one can force your consent. People can force you to say yes, because they have more power, through the ability to punish, or by making threats. But no one can force you to *consent*. Nor can you force anyone else to consent. It has to be given freely. Even given freely, many things impact our ability to both give *and* receive consent. We'll talk about the issues of capacity, knowledge, agreement, and autonomy in Chapters 2-5.

Consent is for everyone: all ages, races, sexes, genders, affiliations, presentations, and any other identity you can think of. Everyone has the right to have their consent respected and upheld.

When you use and respect consent you create safer spaces where people can be open and honest. People can be themselves because they're able to give an honest answer to any request. This makes their yes that much more authentic, because they understand they also have the power to say no and know that it will be respected; they could even change their mind, or say, "Stop," and that would still be okay. People can set boundaries, and expect those boundaries to be respected.

Respecting someone's consent includes many things. It can mean asking before doing, and then waiting for an answer. It can mean accepting an honest yes when you hear one, and accepting any type of no without question or push-back. Throughout the book we're going to show what this looks like through stories and examples.

This type of space—a space where consent is freely given and consistently honored—creates consent culture. Consent culture exists when people asking for consent is a normal, expected behavior. People ask before doing, and respect the response given. Consent culture is a condition where a person's autonomy—their right to make decisions about their own body, mind, and spirit—is upheld by everyone around them.

Over time, we create a world where people know they can say yes to the things they want, no to the things they don't, and people will respect and honor those answers. This is where consent starts, and the place we will begin our discussion of this complex topic. This is where we begin to change the world.

Consent is a difficult, emotional, and evolving topic. There is a lot to unpack and process. Each chapter includes questions and exercises to help you explore. We've included stories and examples to read along the way, and have done our best to include a diverse body of experiences and identities. We hope you see yourself in these pages, and discover what consent means to you. We're not going to get to everything, but hope this serves as a good start.

Without a clear basis for understanding, things get muddled. People believe they understand what consent is, and they act from that understanding. What we've found, through our teaching and exploration, is that most people either don't understand consent well, or have different concepts of what consent should be—a sure recipe for problems.

Imagine a situation where one person grows up in a community where everyone hugs all the time. This is normal, comfortable, and expected behavior. Now imagine another person grows up in a community where it's normal to keep one's distance and maintain personal space. A family in the latter community would ask before touching. The act of hugging might be seen as intimate, maybe even sexual.

What happens when people from these two communities meet for the first time? At best, there is confusion and awkwardness. At worst, there is an act of assault. Whatever your personal opinion, you can see how the different understandings of "normal" creates a problem. A better understanding of consent helps to first identify and then talk about the problem; hopefully before it happens.

⌄

We have seen a lot of evidence over the course of many years of study and education on this subject to suggest that consent makes things better. Consent culture helps to set good expectations. It helps people recognize when they are respected. Practiced well and consistently, consent creates spaces where people can open up and explore, fostering safety and trust.

When we practice consent, we act in direct opposition to rape culture and a world where people believe it's okay to take things without permission. Consent culture is set against the idea that anyone has the "right" to something because they are either strong enough to take it, or lucky enough to not get caught. Instead, we build a world where asking for consent—before doing something—is normal.

For many, that's not the world we live in, but we're moving in that direction. This book is a part of that.

⌄

When we started the Consent Academy, we wanted to understand consent better, and teach people what we learned. Eventually, it became clear that we could only reach a limited number of people in person. There are many reasons for this. Primarily, we recognized that not everyone learns well in workshop settings. Additionally, not everyone could easily get to Seattle to learn directly from us. Finally, there just weren't enough of us.

This book, and the concept of consent, is for everyone. Years ago, when we sat down to figure out what consent meant to us and how to teach it, we never imagined the journey would lead us to writing this book. These pages hold some of the basics we discovered. We wanted to share all of the complexity, difficulty, wonder, struggle, laughter, and tears we encountered throughout the journey. Unfortunately, that wouldn't all fit.

What follows is our best attempt to share the basics. We have collected concepts and ideas that form the building blocks of what we have come to believe is crucial to the concept of consent. This isn't a book to tell you how to practice consent. It is a book to help you understand what consent is, so you can practice in your own life.

To get the most out of the Consent Primer, try the following:

- o Read through to find new concepts and ideas.
- o Practice the exercises, and give honest answers to the questions.
- o Find the places consent fits into your life.
- o Look for how you can improve your practice of consent.
- o Be brave. Some of this may be difficult.
- o Practice your self-care. Take a break if you need it.
- o And challenge yourself to look at consent in a new way.

Consent is an amazing and wonderfully complex topic. It has been the foundation of our work and our lives since we started this journey. And we know there is so much more to come. Join us, and together we can change the world.

- Volunteers of the Consent Academy

Skill Building: Beginnings

Before you get started on the rest of the book, take a minute to try to answer the following questions. (Don't worry if you aren't sure exactly what this exercise is asking; just answer the prompts to the best of your current ability.)

How do you define consent for yourself right now?

_____

_____

_____

_____

What is an example of consent I gave someone today?

_____

_____

_____

_____

What is one time you received consent from someone today?

_____

_____

_____

_____

What is an example of a time you wish someone had asked for consent?

_____

_____

_____

_____

Describe a time someone else listened to you and respected your consent.

_____

_____

_____

_____

Describe a time you respected someone else's consent.

_____

_____

_____

_____

_____

_____

_____

What do you want to know about consent?

_____

_____

_____

_____

_____

_____

_____

Chapter 1: Why Talking About Consent is Important

As you might guess, we believe talking about consent is enormously important. We did write a book, after all. We want to help people better understand and use consent as part of their daily lives. To talk about why it's important, we've broken it down into sections.

We Don't Talk About Consent Enough

When did you first learn about consent? We're not asking about the first time someone respected your consent, or the first time you respected someone else's consent. We want you to think about the first time someone sat down and taught you what consent was, what it looked like, how to give it, and how to receive it.

Write down what you remember:

_____

_____

_____

_____

It might have been when you were young; maybe a parent or caregiver told you about consent as part of "the talk" about sex. If so, you had a jump start. Call that person after you've finished this chapter and thank them!

It might have been when you were in school; there are a handful of health or sex-ed classes that include consent as part of their curriculum. Recent research shows that about 14-16% of people learned something about consent in middle school. High schools are a little better, coming in at 21-25%.[1] They don't often talk about it in detail, but consent at least gets mentioned.

You might have first discussed consent in college, or in a class you took as an adult. Many college campuses have been talking about consent as a way to reduce rape and sexual assault. This is important because 25% of women and 7% of men report unwanted sexual incidents while attending college.[2]

---

[1] PPFA Consent Survey, Planned Parenthood, 2015 - www.plannedparenthood.org/files/1414/6117/4323/Consent_Survey.pdf

[2] College Sexual Assault, Anderson, Nick & Clement, Scott, The Washington Post, 6/12/2015 - https://www.washingtonpost.com/sf/local/2015/06/12/1-in-5-women-say-they-were-violated

Perhaps you discovered information about consent for the first time on the internet, maybe in a blog post or a video. There's a lot of good content out there—and some bad, as well. If the internet was your first introduction, we hope you found knowledgeable content.

Maybe this book is the first time you're learning about consent. If so, welcome. We hope you find what you need.

Whenever the first time was, did it feel like enough information? Did you come away from the conversation thinking, "I get this consent thing, and I know how to handle myself," or something similar?

If our experience has taught us anything, it's that feeling confident about consent is the exception rather than the rule. Most people come away from talking about consent the first time feeling confused. Even worse, sometimes they come away thinking that they know what they're doing, when they don't.

Story: I Thought I Knew

A young man, we'll call him Bill, was on a high school trip to Edinburgh, Scotland. The chaperones and teachers had talked to the students about staying respectful and careful while abroad. As a senior, Bill thought he was able to take care of himself.

He also thought of himself as careful with the young women he'd dated.

"My health teacher talked about getting consent before sex. And I always asked if it was okay to do more than make-out. I thought I knew what to do."

One night, a bunch of the students snuck out of the hostel and went down to the local pub. Many were 18 and able to buy alcohol, although Bill was not. While they sat, scared that one of their chaperones might come in, a group of women from the nearby college joined them.

Bill tried to refuse the first beer, but gave in as his friends urged him to "join the party." After the first, the second was harder to refuse. When one of the women starting making out with him, Bill felt lucky and flattered.

Three beers later, Bill could hardly think straight. The woman asked him to walk her home, even though he knew nothing about the city. Then she asked him to come "up for a lark" (which means "just for fun"). When she started undressing him, he tried to say no. Drunk, confused, and in an unfamiliar place, Bill asked her to stop, but she didn't.

The next morning Bill woke up on the steps of a building he'd never seen, unsure of when he'd even left her apartment. Hungover and missing half his clothes, he made it back to the school group. He lied, telling them he'd been mugged.

"No one ever told me I needed to give consent, or that I should be careful around alcohol. My mom told me half a dozen times to make sure I listened when a girl said no, but no one ever told me what to do if she didn't listen to me. Hell, no one even mentioned I might not want to have sex.

"I was so embarrassed. I couldn't tell my parents, my girlfriend, or even my friends what happened. I knew they would hate me, or laugh at me, or tell me to just get over it. It took me years before I could date again. And when I did, I froze the first time we tried to have sex.

"But she didn't laugh, and she didn't hate me. I told her about that night, and she encouraged me to get help. It took awhile, and some therapy, but I can finally talk about what happened."

Bill's story may surprise you. Would it be less surprising if we changed the name to Barbara and had her meeting a man at the pub? How did it feel to read the story? What would you have done?

Read back through and ask yourself, "Where was the first consent problem?" If you answered, "When the students snuck out," you would be correct. They had consented to stay in for the night, and didn't uphold that agreement.

How about the second consent problem? Bill said no to the first beer, and his friends pressured him into taking it. Never pressure someone after they say no. Peer pressure is something we've all fallen victim to at some point. To be clear, though, taking the beer doesn't make what happened later Bill's *fault*.

We would argue that another problem was Bill's lack of consent education. How to give consent was something he needed to understand and practice. He was taught to *ask* for consent in sexual situations, but hadn't been taught to *give* consent too. Being coerced or forced into something wasn't okay, and he had the right to say no.

We don't talk about consent enough, and we don't teach enough of it. Too many people go into an interaction with another person and don't know how to state their boundaries, or even how to give an honest yes. Consent is something that needs to be learned, talked about, and practiced.

Consent is Complex

We've said this before and we will say it again: consent is complicated. In order to understand it, we need to be able to talk about and work with it.

We have often heard:

o   Consent is simple, we don't need to talk about it.

o   It's easy: you just say yes when you want something, and no when you don't.

o   If everyone would just say no when they don't want something, everything would be fine.

o   I don't need to learn about consent—I know when someone is uncomfortable.

o   Consent is only about sex, so it should just be part of sex-ed.

o   You just know if they want something or not.

We disagree with *all* of these.

Consent, at its core, is an agreement between two or more people to engage willingly in an activity. You engage in hundreds of these types of interactions every day. You may not think of them in terms of consent, but consent is always present. This can happen explicitly (when you make a direct request and get a direct answer) or implicitly (when you're both working from the same conceptual framework and agree without saying anything).

Given the above statements, and the number of interactions a person engages in on an average day, consent becomes complex simply by its frequency. And that's before we get into issues of understanding, capacity, power differentials, oppression, privilege, cultural differences, community differences, and dozens of other factors. All of these contribute to how consent is understood, practiced, responded to, and upheld.

Consent is complicated. The more we discuss it, encourage it, and work on it, the better we get at doing it.

Consent is a Skill that Needs to be Practiced

Ever try to learn a new skill? Riding a bike? Tennis? A second language? A new job? Learning new things is something we start doing before we're even born, and keep doing throughout our lives. Once we learn a new skill, we have to practice it, to both keep what we've learned, and to get better at it.

Consent is no different. It's a skill, or set of skills, that once learned, will help keep you and others safe. The more you practice these skills, the easier they become. The easier they are, the more room you have to learn more.

As you read through this book you will learn this set of skills. If you learn a skill, and never practice it, that skill will disappear. On the other hand, if you practice a skill, it will both improve, and eventually it will become so automatic that you barely need to think about it any more.[3]

Let's imagine this is a book on juggling. The first skill would be throwing a ball into the air and catching it. (That may sound like an oversimplification, but it's actually true: you can't learn to juggle until you how how to throw and catch a ball.) Next, we could explain how to grip the ball, toss the ball, and catch the ball. We could explain what to watch, and how to respond to a problem (for instance, what to do if you consistently drop the ball in a particular way). Then we could explain the next set of skills you would need--like maybe good peripheral vision or endurance in the muscles of your hands--and how to go about building those skills.

Over time, and with practice, you would learn how to juggle. You would make mistakes along the way. There would be a lot of dropped balls. There might be some cursing or laughter, but you would get better.

Consent is the same. This book will teach you basic concepts and skills to get started. You will make mistakes along the way. There will be miscommunication and missed opportunities. There may even be some cursing or laughter. With practice, you will get better.

Let's start with two basic skills.

Skill Building: Saying Yes

Start with thinking about something you want. It can be anything from pizza, to sex, to a new car. Pick something with some feeling or energy behind it.

Close your eyes (after reading the rest of the instructions) and imagine someone (an actual person) offering you the thing you want.

Say, "Yes," out loud.

(It needs to be out loud. Saying it in your head doesn't count.)

How did it feel to say, "Yes," to something you wanted?

_____

_____

There are many ways to say yes. What might be another way you could indicate you agree to the offer?

_____

_____

Try the most enthusiastic yes you can think of giving. How does that feel different?

_____

_____

How would your yes change if the person you are saying it to is different (maybe a different age, race, sex, or gender than the person you originally imagined)?

_____

_____

_____

What about a lackluster or unsure yes? How does that feel different?

_____

_____

Skill Building: Saying No

Now think about something you *don't* want. It can be anything from pizza, to sex, to a new car. Pick something with some feeling or energy behind it.

Close your eyes and imagine someone (an actual person) offering you that thing.

Say, "No," out loud.

(It needs to be out loud. Saying it in your head doesn't count.)

How did it feel to say, "No," to something?

_____

_____

There are many ways to say no. What might be another way you could indicate you refuse the offer?

_____

_____

Try the most enthusiastic (or stern) no you can think of giving. How does that feel different?

_____

_____

How would your no change if the person you are saying it to is different (maybe a different age, race, sex, or gender)?

_____

_____

_____

What about giving a lackluster or unsure no. How does that feel different?

_____

_____

What might you do if your no is ignored?

_____

_____

_____

It may seem like saying yes or no is something people do all the time. You might think you don't need to practice it. But you do!

Many people have difficulty giving a clear yes or no when asked.[4] Well documented in both psychology and business, humans have a hard time when asked to give a definite response. We tend to delay our response, or not answer at all. This is especially true if we're afraid our answer is the opposite of what the other person wants. The higher the stakes, the harder it is.

The skill of saying yes or no is one of the foundations of our ability to agree or set boundaries (more on that in Chapter 4). Give it a few thousand repetitions, and you'll be tossing out enthusiastic yeses and strong nos like a champion.

This is just one skill linked to consent. The good news, each one builds on the others. Get better at saying no, and you will get better at holding boundaries. The practice of one skill will help you do better in other areas.

As you go through the rest of this book, look for things you already know how to do. Practice those to get better. Remember that you may need to practice things you already know, as well as things that are new to you.

Consent Increases Safety

We mentioned this before, and it's worth spending more time on: practicing consent helps to create greater safety for everyone. This isn't about making things safer for one group while reducing safety for others. When people work together to grow a consensual space, everyone is safer.

Imagine you're out with friends having a good time. You're enjoying yourself, when someone comes up behind you and gives you a hug. You didn't know someone was there. You don't know who it is. And you didn't give permission to be touched.

What would your reaction be? Be honest, it's just us here.

At best, people are startled and uneasy until they figure out what's going on. Many are shocked, and their body automatically freezes—a fear response. Sometimes people feel violated (See Chapter 5 on autonomy), and get angry or panic. None of these reactions lead to a sense of safety.

We've heard it argued, "It's just a hug. It's no big deal."

This negates the experience of the person whose feeling of safety has been compromised. Negation is a tactic people use when something makes them uncomfortable, like another person responding in an unexpected way. If we believe the ignoring of consent is "no big deal," then the behavior (in response to our violation of their consent) is less harmful to us. We try to make the violation of consent non-threatening. But we can't dictate another person's experience just because we find their response discomforting. They still get to have their experience, whether we like it or not.

Now imagine the same scenario. You're out having a good time with friends and someone comes up to you, where you can see them, and asks if you want a hug. The request might be verbal or nonverbal. It could be relaxed or pushy. You might have some feeling of confusion or social anxiety. But whatever the context, as long as you're able to give an honest answer to the request, and expect the person will respect that answer, you still feel safer than you did in the previous scenario.

This is what consent does. The act of making a request of someone and giving them the opportunity to give an honest answer creates safety. We know we can engage if we choose to, and that we are empowered to make that choice.

Consent makes things safer for both the person giving the response and the person making the request. Let's stick to our hugging example. You come up to someone and give them a hug without asking. Maybe they're happy about it. Maybe they're uncomfortable. Maybe they're scared. Maybe they panic. Any of those responses may result in you (the person doing the hugging) being unintentionally hurt—the person receiving the hug may react by defending themselves physically, and push you away, or give you an elbow to the stomach. Without asking, you don't know if they want it or not. You might have a good guess, but you can't be sure. And you certainly can't be sure of how they will react.

When you ask, and get an honest response, you know it's okay to proceed, or if you need to back off. You've told the person what you want, waited for them to answer, listened to the answer, and respected it. You can feel good about your behavior as you demonstrate respect for the person's choice. You also build trust between yourself and the person you asked.

There's no need to feel defensive. There's no need to worry about how the behavior will be received. As long as you both have the capacity to both give and receive consent (Chapter 2), enough information to make a decision (Chapter 3), a clear agreement (Chapter 4), and the autonomy to do it (Chapter 5), you have consent. When you know the other person wants the same thing as you, you feel safer.

This applies to hugs, sex, work situations, taking pictures, holding the door for someone, and a thousand other things, both physical and non-physical. There is opportunity to create safer environments everywhere.

Consensual interaction between people creates safety. Safety creates connection. Connection creates more authentic interaction and trust. Authenticity creates more opportunity for consent. It's a positive feedback loop that leads to a better world for everyone.

Skill Building: A Consensual Hug

Since we've been talking about consent-based hugging, here is one way to do that:

When you're the person giving or requesting the hug:

1. Make sure you want to give a hug.

2. Approach the person where they can see you.

3. Wait until they see you. Direct eye contact is best.

4. Ask verbally, "Would you like a hug?"

5. Ask nonverbally, by extending your arms to the sides, open as though to hug, with your palms facing towards the person. Do this *without* stepping forward.

6. Wait for a response.

7. If they say, "Yes," verbally (or another acceptance word or phrase, like, "Okay," or, "Sure"), or mirror your nonverbal request, step forward and hug them.

   o   It is best to start with a short (2-3 seconds), social hug. If you feel them get tense, stiff, or squirmy, stop and back off.

8. If they say, "No" (or another boundary setting phrase, like, "No, thanks," or "Not right now"), or give a nonverbal signal like wrapping their arms around their body, step back and acknowledge them. Say, "Okay," "No worries," "Cool," or something else that lets them know that you will honor their choice.

   o   Avoid commenting on their choice, asking why, or trying for more contact. It's okay if they don't want a hug.

9. If they don't say anything or you can't read their body language, *assume that the answer is* **no**.

When you're the person receiving or accepting the hug:

1. Notice when someone approaches you and makes either a verbal or nonverbal request.

2. Ask yourself if you honestly/authentically want a hug from that person.

3. If you want the hug say, "Yes," or "Sure," or give some other affirmative statement, and/or mirror their nonverbal request (meaning that you reflect their body-language of extended, open arms). Step forward into the hug.

   a.   Remember: you can stop hugging at any time.

   b.   If you want out of the hug, or if you're feeling uncomfortable, stop hugging them and let go.

   c.   If needed, tell the other person, "Enough," or, "Stop," and push against them.

4. If you don't want the hug say, "No," "No, thank you," "Not today," or some other negation statement, and give a nonverbal sign like crossing your arms or clasping your hands.

   o   If the person continues to ask or gets pushy, leave the situation or ask for help.

This may not apply to every situation, but you can practice these skills as part of your greater consent toolbox.

To See When it's Being Broken or Violated

The process we've just gone over might feel awkward at first, but it helps. The practice of consent starts with awareness. As you work with consent and integrate it into your life, it becomes more familiar and comfortable. With integration comes an awareness of others, their practice of consent, and consensual behaviors. When we know how to approach someone for a consensual hug, we become aware when others are *not* doing the same. This is true of all consensual activity. The more we practice, the more we notice.

Not everyone is willing or able to practice good consent, however. When you see someone not listening to boundaries, avoiding honest requests, disrespecting autonomy, or ignoring consent, then you know who to avoid (or who might benefit from reading this book).

The more people you have in your life who are able to practice and affirm consent, the lower your risk of engaging with someone who will violate your consent. The more aware of consensual behavior you are, the more you're able to enforce your boundaries. The more you practice consent with other people, the more they will understand the need to practice consent with you.

By understanding consent and its practice, we become sensitized to it. We start to expect it as part of our life, and we reduce the risk of interacting with people who would break it.

To Speak Up for Your Own Wants and Needs

Part of practicing consent is being aware of what you want or need, and knowing your boundaries. That awareness comes from experience, practice, and introspection. It also helps to have time to consider what you think or how you feel about something before giving an answer.

Many of us have difficulty knowing our needs and desires. Sometimes this is because we grew up thinking our wants were unimportant or would never get fulfilled. Sometimes it's because we've been encouraged to put the wants or needs of others in front of our own. Sometimes it's just because we've never put a lot of time or energy into exploring them.

Your needs and desires are important. They're vital to understanding how to answer a request. Do you want a hug? Would you like pizza for dinner? Are you up for intercourse tonight? How you answer a request comes—at its best—from the honest awareness of what you want or don't want.

Even when you have awareness, it can be hard to say either yes or no. You might be concerned about the other person, fear rejection, or not know the right thing to say. There are many reasons people have a hard time giving a clear answer.

Using consent, you get a lot of opportunity to practice both thinking about what you want, and giving an honest answer. It may be hard at first but it will get easier.

"What if you're not sure?" We get this question a lot. It's okay to be uncertain. There are times when you don't have a strong preference one way or the other. (If you honestly don't have a preference, you can always flip a coin.) There are also times when you just don't know. It may be you need more time to think or feel about it.

Imagine if someone asks, "Would you like to go geocaching with me?" It might be something you've done before, and you may already have a yes or no answer. It might be the first time someone asked you to do it, and you'd need more time to think about it. Maybe you don't know what it is, and don't know if it's something you want or not. (Geocaching is a real-world, outdoor treasure hunting game, using GPS-enabled devices.

Participants navigate to a specific set of GPS coordinates and then attempt to find the geocache (container) hidden at that location.)

When you're not sure if you want something, it's okay to say so. It doesn't mean yes and it doesn't mean no. Tell the person asking, "I need more time to think about it," or, "I'm not sure. Let's hold off for now." Don't say you want something until you know. Take time to think, feel, ask more questions, and figure it out.

Using consent is a great way to practice speaking up for your desires. Start small if it feels difficult, but keep practicing. It will get easier.

To Honor the Wants and Needs of Others

In the same way consent helps you to speak up for yourself, it also helps you to honor when others speak up for themselves. If they say yes, then that's great: they have agreed to your request. If they say no, that's also great: they've upheld their boundaries, and you know to not proceed.

Learning to accept an honest answer is also a skill. If the person agrees, it can seem easy. But sometimes we think we want something, only to find we're unsure when someone actually gives it to us. Sometimes we may have wanted something at one point in time, but later on we find that we don't anymore. The desire might have been fulfilled, or it may have faded over time. Imagine you have a desire for ice cream. You might start off wanting one flavor when you go into the store, but once there you find thirty other flavors. All of a sudden you're no longer craving pistachio, you want mango.

Learning to accept an honest no is hard. When we want something, and ask for it, we become invested in the answer. How invested we are determines how much of an emotional reaction we're likely to have. If you care a little, hearing or seeing a no might seem fine. If you care a lot, hearing or seeing a no might feel devastating.

You may have all kinds of different feelings about the other person's answer. It's important to note that having them is ok and *normal*. When we want something and are told no, we can feel hurt, rejected, angry, or ashamed. There's nothing wrong with this. However, acting on those feelings without thinking can be harmful. It is the *behaviors* you do in *response* to your feelings that have the most impact. Being angry when someone says no might be understandable. Projecting anger onto them (by raising your voice in your response to their answer, for example) is not acceptable.

If someone says no to a request you make, the best response is to say, "Thank you." Give them positive feedback for setting and holding their boundaries. Holding boundaries is hard work, and it's important (and powerful) to honor people for doing hard work.

To Recover from Mistakes

We all make mistakes. It's part of being human. Sometimes the mistakes are tiny. Sometimes they're massive. When we practice consent regularly, we build stronger connections and more trust with people. Trust helps people to know we have a positive intent towards them. Knowing that, they are more likely to be understanding.

When it comes to consent, everyone makes mistakes. Everyone breaks or violates consent. Most of these breaks are so small we barely notice them. Maybe you starting talking to someone on the bus when they wanted to be left alone. These types of things happen as part of everyday life due to inattention, lack of knowledge, or competing desires. They are part of relationships and being human.

Some are much more severe. They create a rift between two people which then needs to be healed. The good news is that these rifts can be repaired if the people involved are willing to work on it.

Story: What Happened to My Car?

Jin and Emry have been friends since the 5th grade. They grew up doing everything together. They went to the same schools, studied music together, and even started a band.

One night, Jin took Emry's car while the band was finishing a 2nd encore. Jin didn't ask. Didn't say anything. Didn't even text. Emry came out, tired after two long sets, to find their car missing. A fan, who'd been out smoking, told how Jin drove away in a hurry.

Emry spent the rest of the night trying to find out what happened. Dozens of calls and texts later, Jin was found around dawn, passed out in front of a local bar.

The yelling from their fight was epic. Jin tried to explain about an ex-girlfriend being at the show, and the panic attack they had because of seeing her. Emry responded by yelling about insensitive friends and irresponsible behavior. Exhausted and worn out, they both ran out of steam. Emry drove home and Jin caught a cab.

Three days later, after cooling down, the two talked. Emry explained how they were afraid something terrible had happened. Jin agreed to never take the car without asking. After a few weeks of strain, the pair got back to their old friendship—though Emry always kept the car key on their person after that.

What could have been the end to a long friendship, due to a breach of consent, was able to be healed. It was hard, and took both Jin and Emry being willing to talk with one another, but they could lean on years of connection and trust to get through it. If, moving forward, they continue to practice consent with one another, the breach will continue to heal, even if it's not forgotten.

Practicing consent regularly allows us to lean on the trust already created to heal significant rifts. Even when we accidentally violate someone's consent, we use the practice of more consent to help repair the violation. Both the trust previously built, and the introduction of more consensual interaction, aid in the rebuilding process.

This isn't true for all situations. There are some breaches and violations too severe to heal. Not all mistakes can be forgiven.

Remember, if you hurt someone—either by action or inaction—their feelings and perceptions matter. You may have had good intent, but the other person gets to decide how severe a breach is to them.

To Grow Consent Culture

The Consent Academy talks about consent: how to do it, what it means, how to practice it, its complexity, and its implications. We do that in order to help people practice it more. It's our thing.

The more people work to understand consent and build their practice of it, the more they will use it. The more they use consent, the more other people will emulate it. As more and more people practice consent, it becomes normal. People start to see consent as something needed and desirable. As that feeling grows, it begins to include even more people and more areas of life. Finally, consent culture, with all its benefits, will be born.

This is the change we wish to see in the world. This is why we believe talking about consent is important.

Chapter 2: Capacity

Consent is not as simple as just saying yes or no to something. Before you can even get to the asking or answering, you need to have the capacity—also known as the *ability*—to engage in consensual activity.

As you read this chapter, think about capacity as a spectrum or scale. People will fall somewhere on that scale, depending on who they are, what's happening around them, and what they've experienced that day. There are no hard and fast rules about capacity, but there are guidelines.

This chapter is about making sure we have both the ability to make an honest request of someone, and the ability to answer that request.

Defining Capacity

When we talk about consent capacity, we're talking about the physical, mental, emotional, and social ability to A) give or receive an honest and voluntary agreement, or B) set or receive an honest boundary for a specific activity.

Basically, before you can do something consensually, you need to be able to genuinely engage with someone. There are a lot of things that impact our ability to do that. When our ability to make a clear and honest decision is reduced, our ability to determine if a given activity is consensual or not is hampered. The more impact something has, the greater the risk that our consent will be violated or that we will violate someone else's consent.

How about an example?

Imagine you want to consensually take someone's picture. First, you need the ability to do so. Next, you need to ask if you can. To answer, the other person needs to have the ability to both understand the request, and know how they feel about having their picture taken. Then, they either give or withhold permission to take the picture. And finally, you need to have the ability to receive that answer.

Let's assume they said yes and you both understood each other; you can then take the picture—assuming you remember to take off the lens cap.

That's a fairly simple interaction, and yet there are still any number of places where capacity might be an issue. What if either of you are drunk? What if one of you is underage? What if one of you is distracted? What if you want to take a nude photo or a picture that shows something embarrassing? What if you have different ideas on where the picture will be posted?

There are places other than consent where you may have encountered the issue of capacity. People often talk about capacity in medical or legal contexts. Have you ever gone to the doctor for treatment or surgery and been asked to sign a document that says you have the capacity to consent to the procedure? Have you ever heard people wondering if a person has the capacity to stand trial for something? It's a concept that comes up frequently.

As a society, we want to know when people have the ability to make decisions for themselves. One example is drinking and driving. In the United States, the legal limit to drive is a blood alcohol concentration of .08%. If you're over that limit, you are considered to be lacking the capacity to safely operate a vehicle, and you can be arrested.

We also talk about age when it comes to capacity. People under the age of eighteen are unable to legally vote, smoke, serve in the military, and many other things. As a society, we have determined that they don't have the capacity to make clear and appropriate decisions about those activities (though many argue the point).

These are just a few examples. Capacity is a concept that can be found in many areas and professions. You've probably encountered many things that help—and also things that reduce or take away—a person's ability to make good or clear decisions.

We can't talk about capacity without talking about when we don't have it. We use three phrases to talk about what happens when a person doesn't have enough capacity to consent:

- o Diminished Capacity: A state where a person is no longer 100% capable of giving consent. This can be anywhere along the spectrum, and may not indicate impairment.
- o Impaired Capacity: A state where a person is no longer capable of engaging in consensual activity. This can fall anywhere along the spectrum for a given individual due to personal variation.
- o Incapacitated: A state where a person is at zero capacity to give or receive consent. This includes states like unconsciousness, incoherence, and other conditions where a person is incapable of making decisions and/or clearly conveying those decisions to others.

There is no specific line where we can say a person has moved from having full capacity, to diminished capacity, to impaired capacity. It's tempting to say, "At X% of capacity, a person is no longer able to give consent." But that's not how it works.

Each person has different levels of capacity and impairment. Those will change daily, hourly, and sometimes by the minute, depending on what the person is doing. This is why communication and awareness are *so important* when it comes to consent.

Having Capacity

Go back to thinking about capacity as a spectrum. On one side you have the complete ability to give and receive consent. On the other side you have zero ability to do so. In the middle is a long stretch of potential capacity and potential diminishment.

One of the most difficult parts of understanding this concept is the variability and ambiguity. Because each person and each situation will be different, capacity will travel back and forth along the spectrum throughout a given day, or even a given interaction. This can make it difficult to figure out if the person you're talking with, and maybe asking consent from, has the capacity to give it to you.

Having enough capacity to give consent means possessing the ability to make clear and thoughtful decisions based on your own wants, needs, and boundaries. It means being free from too much pressure (by which we mean pressure that would cause you to deviate from your own wants, needs, and boundaries). It also means having enough self-awareness to know when you shouldn't be making a decision.

Maintaining enough capacity to receive consent means having the ability to be consciously aware of what the other person is saying or showing. It means being free of too much pressure or distraction. It means having enough self-awareness to know when you're not able to pay attention to someone else.

Everyone experiences different things that help let them know when they are feeling good about something. Sometimes it's a sense or intuition. Sometimes it's a feeling of confidence, pride, or sureness. Sometimes it's a phrase or series of thoughts. Sometimes it's an analysis of what's going on.

Example: Imagine someone has offered you a new job. It's a good job, but you have some concerns about the workload, and you want to give your potential employer the most well-considered answer that you can. You ask for time to think, and wait until the following morning, when you're well-rested, have eaten a good breakfast, and have taken time to consider the pros and cons of the situation. When you answer, you feel confident with your decision and can give a clear and honest response.

There are ways to improve your confidence. Practicing self-awareness and/or mindfulness helps you learn more about your personal capacity. Because it's such a variable state, it takes time and repetition to learn how to evaluate it. Practice can include breathing exercises, meditation, journaling, self-analysis, perception-checking, honest communication with others, and daily self-reflection.[5] [6]

How do you know when you have enough capacity? Name three things that tell or show you when you're confident and sure of something:

_____

_____

_____

What is it about these three things that help you know that you're sure of something?

How do you know when the person with whom you're interacting has enough capacity? Start with this exercise. Name three things that tell or show you when someone else is being honest and open with you:

_____

_____

_____

What is it about these three things that help you know when another person is being clear and honest?

---

[5] Kabat-Zinn, J. (2006) *Mindfulness for Beginners*. Boulder, CO: Sounds True, Inc

[6] Kabat-Zinn, J. (2013) *Full Catastrophe Living (Revised Edition): Using the Wisdom of Your Body and Mind to Face Stress, Pain, and Illness*. New York, NY: Bantam Books

Remember, we're talking about enough capacity to be clear, open, and honest. For most people, being a little tired won't remove their ability to give consent. There will be some for whom fatigue causes significant diminishment, and may interfere with clear thinking and awareness.

People show capacity in different ways. The longer you know someone, the more you'll understand their cues for when they're present, self-aware, and confident. When you meet someone for the first time you will want to take more time to determine their capacity.

Here are some things to help determine capacity in another person (not a complete list):

- Clarity: When the person communicates, they do so clearly. The communication is appropriate for the situation. It's easy to understand both what they're communicating and what is meant by it.
- Consistency: The person's communication stays the same over time. Phrases used and stories shared stay similar and ring true. The person's behavior is both the same over time, and appropriate to the situation.
- Connective Physical Cues: The person makes regular eye contact. They have an open body posture. They maintain a comfortable distance. They respond when you say something.
- Positive Circumstance: The things happening around the other person favor capacity. There are few distractions, the person isn't intoxicated, they've had enough sleep, etc.
- Open Statements: The person shares openly about their thoughts, feelings, and internal state. When asked about how they're doing they give clear and honest statements that match what you see.

It's always going to be your best guess. We can never fully know what's going on inside another person. Do what you can to determine their level of capacity. If at any point you're uncomfortable or unsure of the other person's capacity, stop.

Lacking Capacity

When anyone in an interaction lacks capacity it means you don't have consent. If either you or anyone in a given interaction lacks the capacity to give or receive consent, consent is not possible and does not exist. If at any point in an interaction a person's capacity becomes impaired, even if they had sufficient capacity to start with, they no longer have capacity, and consent does not exist. Without capacity, consent does not exist.

It may seem like we don't need to state this so many times, but we do. This is a fundamental part of understanding consent and how to work with it.

Story: Compounding Factors

Sam had a long day. He hadn't slept well, worked a 10 hour shift, worked through lunch, and just found out a childhood friend had died. Feeling sad and exhausted, and against his better judgement, Sam got together with friends for a "friendly game night."

Things started to go downhill from the beginning. Sam was given a beer as soon as they came through the door and followed by another when that one was empty. Normally two beers wouldn't have been a problem, but the alcohol, lack of food, exhaustion, and grief worked to leave Sam's head fuzzy and out-of-sorts.

When someone suggested making the card game "more interesting" by betting with real money, Sam knew it wasn't a good idea, but everyone else was playing. So...

Three hours and $250 dollars later, Sam mumbled an apology and left, feeling taken advantage of, and trying to figure out how to make rent.

Sam wasn't in a place to make clear decisions. It would have been better to refuse the second beer, say no to playing for money, and instead, go home and sleep. Also, Sam's friends should have noticed the lack of capacity, and either sent Sam home, or opted to play for chips instead of actual money.

If anyone involved in an interaction doesn't have capacity or loses capacity, consent does not exist and you need to stop whatever it is you're doing.

As in Sam's story, it's rarely just one thing that reduces capacity to the point that someone becomes impaired. It's often a series of things—physical, and /or emotional, and/or social—that pull a person down the capacity spectrum to the point where they become either impaired or incapacitated. We are accustomed to stories about people who become drunk or stoned to the point they are unable to make good decisions. That does happen, but much of the time there are a number of contributing factors that reduce a person's capacity, little by little, until they no longer have the ability to consent.

How do you know when you have lost the capacity to consent? Start with this exercise. Name three things that tell or show when you're no longer able to make good decisions:

_____

_____

_____

Everyone has different internal cues to help them know when they are getting into a bad situation. When we get to the point of no longer being able to determine what we want, or when we're no longer able to hold our boundaries, it's a good sign we've lost the capacity for consent. At that point, the best thing we can do is leave the situation and engage in self-care.

Self-care is taking time to recognize what you need to calm and restore your mind, body, and spirit. It can include many things, but the foundations include a good night's sleep, regular exercise, taking time for yourself, and eating in a way that is good for your body. Self-care improves physical, mental, and emotional capacity.

If you can't leave the situation immediately, fall back on saying no and refusing to give consent. Do what you can to create distance and protect yourself. Where possible, engage someone you trust for help.

To add to the difficulty, the same things that reduce capacity for consent also tend to reduce the ability to have clear and effective communication. The best way to deal with this goes back to self-awareness. The more aware you are, the more likely you are to catch a problem early or identify patterns. The best way to prevent yourself from becoming impaired is to notice when your capacity is starting to diminish. Once you notice the diminishing, you can either do things to improve capacity, stop doing things that reduce capacity, or both.

Remember, as your capacity diminishes, your risk of either committing a Consent Violation or having one committed against you goes up: the less capacity you have, the greater your risk.

How do you know when someone else has lost the capacity to consent? Start with this exercise. Name three things that tell or show you when a person with whom you're interacting is no longer able to make good decisions:

_____

_____

_____

What is it about these three things that help you realize there's a problem?

Here are some things that can help you determine a lack of capacity for consent. (**Note:** this is not a complete list; also, physical indicators may be subtle or hidden in some cases, and in other cases these things may just be personality quirks. Use your best discretion.)

- o **Lack of Clarity:** Someone who is having trouble articulating their words, is difficult to understand, or is saying things out of context may have some level of diminished capacity.
- o **Lack of Consistency:** Someone whose behavior doesn't match what they're saying may have some level of diminished capacity. Watch for stories or statements that change over time.
- o **Evasive or Deceptive Statements:** Someone who is lying, trying to avoid answering questions, attempting to distract from the topic at hand, or trying to shift blame to someone or something outside themselves (avoiding responsibility for their actions) often has some level of diminished capacity.
- o **Avoiding Eye-Contact:** If a person is avoiding direct eye-contact, repeatedly looks away from your eyes after very brief eye-contact (a second or less), or is often looking at the floor or ceiling, this may indicate high levels of anxiety, or some other kind of diminishment in capacity.
- o **Noticeable Impairment:** Someone who appears drunk, stoned, or intoxicated (look for things like slurred or very slow speech, droopy eyelids, uncoordinated or clumsy movement, etc.) has some level of diminished capacity.
- o **Significant or Extreme Emotional States:** Someone who is having a strong emotional reaction has some level of diminished capacity. Things to look for here might include (but are not limited to) changes in the volume of someone's voice (speaking more loudly or quietly than they normally do, or than is appropriate for the environment), speaking more quickly than they normally do, or body language changes or tics (like wringing hands, facial tics, or crossing arms and/or legs). **Note:** this is true for many kinds of emotions, not just the ones we think of as "negative emotions," like sadness or anger; extreme happiness, or other emotions we think of as "positive," can still sometimes indicate reduced capacity.
- o **Problematic Circumstances:** Environments where there is significant substance use (drugs, alcohol, etc.), high levels of distraction (lots of people in the room, etc.), significant emotional impact (a break-up conversation, recent car accident, family death, etc.), or any other circumstance that might impair someone is likely to create some level of diminished capacity.

In trying to determine a person's capacity, it's important to remember that you will be making your best guess. It can be hard to know for sure if someone has the ability to consent or not, especially when you're dealing with some form of complex diminishment where they are being impacted by multiple things at the same time that lower their capacity. There are a couple things you can do.

The first, and best, thing to do is probably also the simplest: just ask them. If you think the person you are interacting with may be impaired, let them know what you're seeing and ask them if they feel comfortable continuing. Let them know you're okay if they're not up to something, and offer to come back to them later after they've done some self-care. They may feel compelled to say yes for the "wrong reasons" if they think that the offer is only available for a "limited time," so make it clear that you're ok with whatever feels most comfortable to them, even if it means "missing out" on an experience.

Secondly, always err on the side of caution. If you have any doubt or confusion, don't do anything that requires the person to give or receive consent. If there is something you want from them, you can always ask again later. Waiting is always better than violating consent, risking harm, and damaging relationships.

There is much to consider when assessing your own or someone else's capacity for consent. Start by reflecting on your day-to-day life, and think about what comes into play in affecting your own capacity most often. Then, one by one, practice assessing those things in the people around you.

Read on for some specific things you can watch for and reflect on.

Things that Diminish Capacity and Increase Risk

There are many things people use, engage in, and encounter that diminish their capacity to give or receive consent. This will vary from person to person. What has a significant influence on one person may have almost no impact on another. Conversely, what seems fine to one person may have a huge impact on someone else.

As discussed earlier, reflect on capacity as a spectrum. Something can diminish capacity without creating impairment or incapacitation. Additionally, any diminishment increases the risk of *both* committing a Consent Violation, *and* having one committed against you. Wherever possible, work to increase capacity and avoid things that diminish it.

Alcohol and Other Impairing Substances

There are many things which can alter the way we think, behave, react, and make decisions. We talk about them in relation to consent because they affect our capacity.

Alcohol is one of the most common examples people tend to discuss, in part because of its prevalence in western culture. Having a drink or two is normal for many people. Where dating and sex are involved, it is even more common for people to think they *need* "social lubrication" or "liquid courage." Alcohol is used by many to lower inhibition and reduce anxiety when it comes to difficult and/or emotional situations.

The risk is that alcohol lowers the ability to be aware, make decisions, and think clearly. Therefore, it diminishes our capacity for consent. It may not remove it entirely, but if we go back to thinking about our "0%-100% spectrum," alcohol can start to pull the level down from 100%, and can lead to impairment and even incapacitation.

Marijuana is another substance which lowers inhibitions, anxieties, and both physiological and emotional responses. Because it lowers awareness, decision-making, and critical thinking, it diminishes the capacity for consent. In addition, marijuana requires special consideration with regards to consent because it is so recently deregulated in many states, more widely available in a greater number of forms than it has been in the past, and less socially accepted than alcohol (so fewer people will know how it affects their bodies).

Almost every drug, regardless of its prescription or legal status, has some impact on the body and the mind. When using a drug, it's important to be aware of and understand how it impacts you, and how it may diminish or affect your capacity for consent. It's also important to consider the amount of something you take. A single beer won't have the same impact as two, three, or six. Half a gram of marijuana won't have the same impact as one gram, two, or more. The more of a substance you take, the greater the impact.

This impact is further affected by how quickly and frequently you take it. Spreading something out over a few hours is going to have a different effect than having it all within twenty minutes. Our bodies also build up a tolerance to most drugs the longer they're taken, so the first interaction with a new substance is going to have a stronger physical effect than the twentieth or fiftieth.

All of this information leads to understanding how a specific substance impacts you and your capacity for giving and receiving consent. It is your responsibility to know how having a couple drinks is going to change your reactions and ability. If it's going to be a big impact, know that and make decisions about your consent before you have those drinks.

When trying something for the first time, you're not going to know how much of an impact it might have. You may have some guesses from watching other people take it, but everyone's body is different. Again, this means defining your consent ahead of time. It's not about ruining the fun, it's about taking responsibility for your own experience and staying safe.

For any of these issues, but more so for intoxicants, there is also the concern of compounded impact. Diminishment in capacity is made up of many things at the same time. Remember the example of Sam and the poker game? Everything you're experiencing adds up to the total impact to your capacity. When you combine alcohol or other substances with physical and emotional issues, these create a greater impact than they would alone. It's important to be aware of how you react to intoxicants in a variety of circumstances.

Remember, you get to decide what you want to do with your body. If you find that taking an intoxicating substance reduces your capacity to give or receive consent, you need to understand that how you take it—or the decision to take it at all—is a choice. It may not always be an easy choice. There are many things that make it hard, but it is still your choice. If you need help regulating or investigating your relationship with intoxicating substances, there are places and people to help you.

Physical Concerns

Anything that impacts your body can diminish your capacity for consent. Our body is a system. What impacts us physically also impacts our thoughts and emotions.

A physical condition most people are familiar with is fatigue or lack of sleep. Have you ever put in a long day at work or school, or had a bad night's sleep? These things tend to leave people feeling tired, out of sorts, and slow. This lack of energy lowers our ability to be aware, make decisions, and think clearly. It diminishes our capacity for consent.

Another issue is lack of food or water. Have you ever skipped a meal, or maybe more than one? Most people feel "off," distracted, or slowed when they don't have enough food in their system. In more serious circumstances, this can lead to a condition called hypoglycemia (low blood sugar) which can cause impairment or even incapacitation. Dehydration (not having enough water in your body) will cause the same problem, but can happen even faster.

Ever had a bad cold or flu? Everyone gets sick from time to time. Some illnesses pass quickly, while others linger or never go away. Some have a significant impact on the body, while others have a mild one. They all take some amount of energy and focus. They all result in some level of diminishment in our capacity for consent.

Pain is another example of something that can have a significant impact. The state of being in pain takes energy, focus, and control. The more pain a person is in, the greater the impact on the body, and thus the greater the impact on capacity. It's also important to note that many of the medications used to treat significant pain can have an additional impact on capacity for consent.

There are many issues that affect the body. Remember, no two people are the same. We experience physical things in different ways. Avoid deciding what someone else is feeling—or the level of impact those feelings might have on them—based on your own experience. Each person gets to decide for themselves how much of an impact something has on them.

Whatever the issue, the impact on our physical self creates an impact on our mental and emotional self, which creates an impact on our ability to give and receive consent. The impact can be minor or significant depending on what's going on. Whether small or large, where there is an impact on our physical self, there is some level of diminished capacity to engage in consent.

Emotional Concerns

We all have feelings. It's part of being human. Experiencing and identifying emotions is normal. From a gentle sense of contentment to raging anger, there is a whole spectrum of feelings we experience as part of moving through the world. These feelings will impact our capacity for consent.

Your current emotional state—how you're feeling in a given moment—has the most significant impact on your capacity. The greater the intensity of the feeling, the more impact it will have on your ability to be aware, make decisions, and think clearly.

Long-term emotional states also have an effect on consent. A feeling that lasts for days, months, or even years will impact your perception and awareness. Long-term emotional states like depression, anger, loneliness, grief, stress, and similar feelings, can act as a drain on emotional and mental resources. These also act as a perceptual filter through which situations and behaviors are viewed.

Relational issues also affect consent. The better your connection and relationship with someone, the more consent capacity you have. The more strain you have in a relationship, the more diminishment you experience in your consent-capacity, because your attention is being given over to other issues. Where there are significant problems, negative emotions, fighting, or abuse, the capacity to give and receive consent can become impaired.

Just like physical issues, no one else gets to define when your feelings are diminishing your capacity. This is something for you to be aware of and understand about yourself. It's not up to you to tell someone else that their feelings are causing problems. Everyone gets to practice emotional awareness for themselves.

When you find your emotions are causing diminishment in your capacity, there are a couple things you can do. One course of action is to wait longer before giving or receiving consent. Emotions can linger after a significant experience. Take time for those feelings to fade before making serious decisions or negotiating. Another avenue is to practice emotional regulation skills, emotional awareness, patience, and relaxation. All of these will help you be aware of when your feelings are draining your emotional resources, and will help you to pause and wait until you're ready to re-engage with someone.

Cognitive Concerns

Just like our emotions, our thoughts and mental capacity have an impact on our consensual self. There are a number of things we experience, both internally and externally, which can cause our capacity to be reduced.

One of the most common diminishments is mental fatigue. Have you ever gotten through a long day or a hard exam and felt like your mind was tired? When we use our brain or intellectual function intensely or for a long period of time, it gets tired. When this happens, we have a harder time being aware and thinking about things, which leads to a diminishment in capacity.

Negative thought loops and recurring problematic thoughts can also lead to reduction in capacity for consent. When we have negative thoughts, either about ourselves or the world around us, the thoughts sometimes get stuck in a repeating cycle, like a broken record. When that happens, it can drain mental resources, and change your perceptions.

Another cognitive issue is traumatic brain injury or TBI. This occurs when the brain is injured due to any kind of bump, blow, or jolt to the head. The effects of TBI are wide and varied. For some they last a short time, and for others the effects can be permanent. When present, these effects often impact cognitive function.

Issues surrounding cognitive function can also impact capacity for consent. Sometimes these are issues a person is born with. Sometimes they are caused by accident, illness, or aging. Like other things in this section, there are a wide variety of expressions and ramifications. These conditions don't take away a person's right to consent, but they may impact the ability to do so.

If you find your cognitive function regularly causes some diminished capacity, be sure to check with a doctor, if you haven't already. Make sure to take more time and give more attention to your decision making in order to compensate. Often giving some space, taking additional time, and asking others for help will mitigate potential consent issues.

Mental Health Concerns

The category of mental health is huge. It covers everything from healthy functioning, to emotional fluctuations, to serious emotional traumas, to life-threatening behavioral issues. Here are a few examples:

- o Depression: A state of feeling down, sad, hopeless, and/or helpless; often includes a loss of interest in activities, a lack of happiness, and a variety of physical symptoms. When someone is depressed, they frequently have trouble making decisions, and may not always act in their own best interest.

- o Anxiety: A state of feeling afraid, irritable, jumpy, worried, and/or distracted; often includes disruptions to normal activities, difficulty concentrating, and a variety of physical symptoms. When someone is anxious, they also frequently have difficulty making decisions and/or staying present, and may become overly-focused on the object of anxiety.

- o Trauma: When someone experiences an event like being attacked, abused, or anything that causes an extreme negative emotional response, it can create a trauma reaction. Think of this as a mental/emotional injury, like breaking a bone or spraining a ligament. That trauma, if not processed properly (like setting a broken bone), can lead to post-traumatic stress disorder (PTSD) which creates long-term difficulties that need to be worked through—often with help (like physical therapy, in the case of bodily injury). When a person has trauma, either recent or previous, it impacts how they react to situations that may remind them of their trauma.

There are many other issues and concerns surrounding mental health. When a mental health concern is present, it will impact capacity. If you or someone you are wanting to give or receive consent to/from has a mental health concern, your first step is to learn how the condition impacts you (or them) and the people around you. Then practice skills to work with or around it to mitigate the consent risk as much as possible. The goal is always to move towards greater health, a better life, and better consent.

Power Differentials

A power differential exists when one person has more power or authority in a situation than another person. Examples include roles like boss/employee, parent/child, teacher/student, mentor/mentee, doctor/patient, police officer/citizen, dominant/submissive, etc. These are roles where one person has more *agency* than another.

Agency is the ability to exert power or influence. A person with a lot of agency can create change. They are able to alter situations to be closer to what they want or need. A person with little agency may be able to create some change in a situation, but not to the same degree or significance, especially when someone with greater agency in involved.

A good example is that of a parent and a child. Young children have very little ability to change things in their lives, unless a parent agrees. The parent has much greater agency and thus the ability to control what the child does or does not do. As the child gets older, their amount of agency grows until, as an adult, the levels of agency equalize between adult children and parents, as reflected by age.

And that is just one example. Our level of agency changes from situation to situation and is influenced by hundreds of different factors. When it comes to consent, the thing to remember is that a person with greater agency has more power in a given situation, and therefore capacity for unbiased or authentic consent between those two people is reduced.

Issues of privilege and oppression create power differentials.[7] A person with privilege innately has more power than someone without that privilege. This is not about what the person does directly—though it can be influenced by behavior—but rather is about the greater agency society and culture *gives* them. Examples of privileged/oppressed groups include men/women, white people/people of color, straight/queer, able-bodied/disabled, and many others. It's important to recognize how privilege can impact power so you can take it into account when looking at capacity—both yours and someone else's.

Other things create power differentials: issues of physical presence (size, state of dress, and appearance), issues of fame or social standing, issues of age or seniority, issues of culture or subculture, or issues of experience—basically anything that sets one person "above" or "ahead" of someone else.

Imagine two people meeting for the first time. One of them is a tall muscular man in an expensive suit. One of them is a short frail woman in a torn dress. Knowing nothing else about them, which would you think had more power? Most people will answer the man. That perception or judgement creates a power differential, and therefore a reduction in consent capacity.

Power differences are not always bad. There are many structures that function by knowing who's in charge and places where it's appropriate for one person to make decisions for someone else (take the parent/child relationship as an example). Power differentials are something we deal with every day. The essential part is being aware of it and how it impacts you.

When one person has more privilege or power than another, they often use that additional agency unconsciously. Where that intersects with consent, it means people will often assume the other person has the same level of ability to say no, even when that isn't true. Thus, they can intentionally or unintentionally coerce a yes from the other person. A coerced or forced yes does not equal consent.

---

[7] Johnson, Allan G. (2006) *Privilege, Power, and Difference 2nd Ed.* Boston, MA: McGraw-Hill

Perhaps you are a manager at your place of work. In that case, you may work with people who have more power than you and people who have less power than you. When making requests of the people you manage, keep in mind that you have more power than they do. That difference in power will affect how they answer. Being conscious of this will help you remember to make requests within that person's scope of duties and abilities. It will also help you phrase your requests in such a way the other person could say no or negotiate for help.

The same is true when interacting with those who have more power. When you are conscious of this power difference, it will be easier to recognize when that person is using their power to get you to agree to something. It will also help you know when you need to exit the situation.

Do your best to understand that these power-differentials exist, and how they can be misused. Make sure you're not misusing them if you are in the position of greater power. Make sure to watch for its misuse when you're in the lesser power position.

Understand that power differentials diminish the capacity for consent. It doesn't automatically create impairment, but the greater the difference in power levels, the greater the impact on capacity, and therefore the greater the chance of a Consent Violation happening.

Significance of the Activity

How significant or important an activity is impacts your ability to consent to it. Has there ever been something you wanted so badly you made problematic decisions around it? Was there ever something you felt was so important that you compromised your own boundaries to make sure it happened? How about doing everything possible to talk someone else into an activity?

The more important something feels, the more likely we are to ignore issues like consent. The emotional and mental attachment to the activity can create "blinders" which make it hard to focus on more subtle things. This lack of awareness combined with a strong emotional need can diminish or impair our capacity for consent.

There are also risks that may come along with the activity itself. Is there a significant risk of injury or harm? Is there anything about the activity itself that can reduce the capacity for understanding or awareness? Is there something that will make it hard to communicate? Is there something that will happen too quickly for you to check in with the other person?

Imagine going spelunking: hiking deep into a cave system. It's dark, cold, and echoing. There is a lot of risk involved, depending on the cave and your equipment. There will be times when it is hard to communicate and difficult to understand someone else when they try to communicate with you. Taking this into account, you would want to establish consent, and a decent plan of action in case something goes wrong, ahead of time.

There are a lot of factors that can make something more risky. That's not always a bad thing. Many people enjoy a bit of risk—skydivers, for example. While consent may still be possible beforehand, it's helpful to recognize what potential issues there might be, and work to reduce the risks as much as possible.

Ways to Mitigate Capacity Risk

Now that we've talked about things that can impact or reduce capacity for consent, let's talk about what you can do to deal with those issues and make things safer. Here are some things to mitigate or reduce both your risk of committing a Consent Violation, and the risk of having one committed against you.

- o **Practice more self-care.** The more rested, stable, and comfortable you feel, the better you will be able to deal with any problems. Practice self-care before, after, and during (if possible) any activity where there's any significant potential for diminishment of capacity.

- **Wait and be patient.** Take extra time to figure things out, analyze the situation, and make your decision. The extra space will help increase your level of capacity.
- **Bring in help.** If you anticipate that your capacity is going to be low, bring in someone else with higher capacity to help make decisions or to let you know when it's time to leave.
- **Negotiate better.** Engage in detailed and explicit negotiations before starting the activity. The more complicated the activity, the more detailed you should try to make the negotiation. If you're not satisfied with the negotiation, don't move forward.
- **Set boundaries.** Boundaries tell other people what's okay and what's not. Set clear, explicit, and understandable boundaries before starting an activity. Ask the other person what their boundaries are.
- **Avoid re-negotiation during the activity.** Avoid trying to figure out if you want or don't want something new while in the middle of something else. Avoid trying to convince someone else to change their mind. Where capacity is lower, especially if it is going to be reduced by the activity itself, it's safer to stick to the original negotiation, or reduce the level of interaction.
- **Be willing to leave the situation.** There are few things that are worth being harmed or harming someone else. Affirm to yourself ahead of time that you are willing to stop what you're doing and walk away; and then, if the situation feels unsafe, or if you find yourself impaired, leave. You can always come back to it, or something similar, later.
- **Make a plan.** Things go wrong; it's a fact of life. Have a plan in your head for what to do if something goes wrong or if you become impaired. If that happens, follow the plan.
- **Ask for help.** If you need more information or perspective, ask someone you trust. If things aren't going well, or if you find yourself heading towards being impaired, ask for help. If you find yourself in a situation where something has already gone wrong and consent has been broken, get help. When you need help, ask for it.

Consent is complex. Your ability to give and receive consent is built on so many different things that it can seem overwhelming. It can seem like there's no way to ever have enough capacity to give consent.

Take heart. You're already using capacity as a gauge, though you might not have realized it. Dozens of times each day you agree or refuse to do something. We use these capacity gauges in social ways, like asking yourself, "Do I want to eat lunch in my office and get more work done, or do I want to take a break and socialize with my co-workers in the lunchroom?" We also use them in physical ways, like when we're internally questioning, "Do I need to use the bathroom right now, or can I complete this task comfortably and then take care of my body's needs?" When a situation comes up, you make a decision on whether or not you feel up to it. You decide if you have the capacity to do it, or even if you have the capacity to make the decision. A real-life example here might be choosing to eat lunch before you have to step into a meeting where you'll be asked to make decisions about next month's ad campaign for a new product line, or other important decisions. That would be a choice to increase your capacity via self-care before you need to make choices about what ads you "consent" to.

Now that you know there is an issue of capacity when it comes to both giving and receiving consent, give thought, care, and examination the next time something comes up. Ask yourself if you feel ready to make the decision. Ask the other person if they feel up to making the decision. If it doesn't feel right, or if it feels too scary, stop until it feels right.

Once you're ready, move on to the next stage of consent: gathering information.

Chapter 3: Informed Consent

As you can already tell, there are many facets to making sure consent is present. The next topic is informed consent. This is the notion that all parties involved in an interaction have the details and information necessary to make a clear and honest decision.

Much like capacity, think about the level of information you have as on a spectrum or scale. How much a person knows or understands will fall somewhere on the scale based on a variety of factors. That understanding will change from interaction to interaction, and sometimes moment to moment.

What is informed consent?

You have probably been exposed to this concept already. Before you accept a job offer, you ask questions about the salary, vacation time, and health benefits. You may ask about the time you need to arrive each morning or the dress code. Before signing your name on the contract, you make sure you know what you are getting into. If you are a hiring manager, you make sure new staff is aware of expectations.

In general, we want to find out more before we commit ourselves to something. We want to know the ins and outs. It may seem like a daunting task, but in truth, we ask for transparency all the time! Have you noticed the additional nutrition information on food menus? What about all of the paperwork you sign when you go in for surgery? These are examples of getting more information to assist in getting consent.

Having informed consent means all sides of an interaction have sufficient information, and understanding of that information, to be able to make an honest and clear decision about engaging in an interaction or not.

Informed consent means knowing what is being requested and the boundaries around that request. It focuses on honest and open communication, and hinges on all parties having enough information to make a decision. Consent cannot exist where there is insufficient information, where there is inaccurate or dishonest information, or where any of the people involved are unable to understand the information.

To help comprehend this concept we will discuss the history of informed consent, how it applies to various aspects of our lives, how to give it, how to get it, and some challenges that might arise.

Informed Consent in Medicine

Looking at the evolution of consent within the medical community can lead to a greater understanding of informed consent in our daily lives. This area, while complex, is something many of us have some experience with. Most people have had to review forms at the doctor's office that explicitly ask for consent.

You have probably heard the phrase, "First do no harm." This is a principle to which many doctors subscribe. The most important thing is to not harm the patient, an example of which is opting to do nothing if a procedure might make the patient worse. This seems straightforward enough, but what the doctors failed to consider was that some patients might not want their help.

In 1914, the Schloendorff v. Society of New York Hospital case went to trial. In this case, a woman named Mary Schloendorff was informed she had a tumor. She made the decision to not go through with removal. The doctors however, failed to listen, and did the procedure against her wishes. Mary developed gangrene after complications. She sued successfully with the judge ruling:

> *Every human being of adult years and sound mind has a right to determine what shall be done with his own body; and a surgeon who performs an operation without his patient's consent commits an assault for which he is liable in damages. This is true except in cases of emergency where the patient is unconscious and where it is necessary to operate before consent can be obtained.*[8]

Although the doctor did what he felt was the responsible action, it was against the wishes of the patient. The patient was not fully consulted and her autonomy was not respected.

Has there been a time in your life when you remember saying you did not want to do something, and your words were ignored? How did you feel?

Sometimes it seems easier to tell people what to do instead of explaining what they need to know. Let's look again at the medical field. In 1957, Salgo v. Leland Stanford Jr. University Board of Trustees came to trial.[9] In this case, a patient, Martin Salgo, woke up paralyzed. He had been put under for a procedure involving x-ray contrast material. Martin said he had never been told that waking up paralyzed was possible.

The doctors wanted to do the right thing and help the patient, but explaining all of the risks might have made the procedure sound terrifying, so they didn't. They gave him a shortened version. For Martin Salgo however, that bit of missing information was crucial and might have impacted his decision to go through with the procedure. He did not have enough information to give consent.

---

[8] Schloendorff v the Society of the New York Hospital, 211 NY 125 105 NE 92 1914 LEXIS 1028 (1914).

[9] Green, Douglas S T, and C Ronald MacKenzie. "Nuances of informed consent: the paradigm of regional anesthesia." HSS journal : the musculoskeletal journal of Hospital for Special Surgery vol. 3,1 (2007): 115-8. doi:10.1007/s11420-006-9035-y

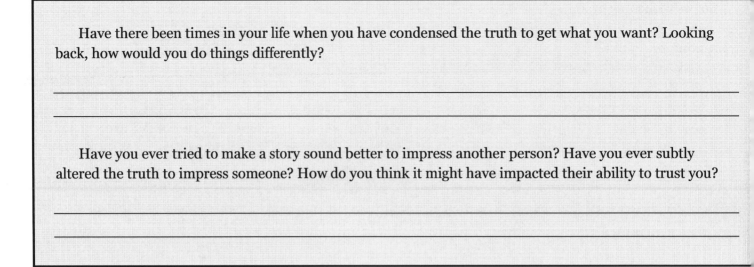

Have there been times in your life when you have condensed the truth to get what you want? Looking back, how would you do things differently?

_____

_____

Have you ever tried to make a story sound better to impress another person? Have you ever subtly altered the truth to impress someone? How do you think it might have impacted their ability to trust you?

_____

_____

It's important that people have enough information to make a fully informed decision. The medical community has found that going against a patient's decision, or not giving them all the information they need to make a decision, can cause harm. The same is true in other consensual interactions.

Informed Consent in Legal History

It might seem simple at this point. Making a decision should be easy if you know what you're agreeing to and believe your decision will be respected. But, what if the situation called for things you didn't understand? What if someone explained every element, but it was too complicated for you to fully grasp? Let's jump over to legal history to examine this.

If you have ever been arrested, or seen someone arrested on television, you might know what the officer will say. That speech is called the Miranda Warning. It informs you of your rights, such as the right to remain silent and the right to have an attorney present while you are being questioned. What you may not have paid attention to is the end. After reading your rights, the officer is required to ask if you understand the rights as they have been explained to you. That last part is crucial!

The Miranda Warning came about after Ernesto Arturo Miranda was arrested in Arizona. At the time of his arrest, he was taken to the police station where officers locked him in a room until they had a written confession. It took the officers only two hours. The confession had some troubling issues, however. On the top of the paper was a paragraph which read, in part, "the confession was made voluntarily, without threats or promises of immunity and 'with full knowledge of my legal rights, understanding any statement I make may be used against me.'"[10] In the confession, Ernesto admitted to kidnapping, rape, and armed robbery.

The confession was not fully informed. He did not understand his rights. His legal team argued that even though his rights were told to him, since he did not understand them, this did not count as being fully informed.

The Supreme Court sided with Miranda. After reviewing the case, it was determined he was not properly informed of his legal rights. The court stated, "The mere fact that he signed a statement which contained a typed-in clause stating that he had 'full knowledge' of his 'legal rights' does not approach the knowing and intelligent waiver required to relinquish constitutional rights."[11]

---

[10] Supreme Court Reporter, "Miranda v. State of Arizona (86 S.Ct. 1602)," June 13, 1966

[11] Cf. Haynes v. Washington, 373 U.S. 503, 512-513 (1963); Haley v. Ohio, 332 U.S. 596, 601 (1948) (opinion of MR. JUSTICE

So, we're making progress towards understanding the significance of informed consent. To give your consent, you need to be fully confident it will be respected, you need to be aware of all aspects to which you are consenting, and you need to be sure you understand what each part means.

Have you ever been asked to stay at work "just a little bit longer" while the boss finished a project or needed help with last-minute changes? She may have told you what the project was, but it might have been hard to agree if you couldn't pin down what "a little bit longer" meant. Did she mean thirty minutes or four hours?

Think of a time when not having a full understanding of a request has come up for you. What was the situation, and how did you handle it?

_____

_____

_____

Informed Consent in Relationships

We've talked about several aspects of informed consent. Now, let's take a look at your daily life and see how informed consent can impact relationships.

When we look at this notion of informed consent within our connections, a number of issues arise. Everyone involved needs to know their consent will be respected, that they are consenting to each part of what they're doing, and that everyone fully understands each part. Likewise, when you ask someone to consent, you need to ensure this is happening. Being explicit and clear will help confirm everyone is aware, in agreement, and signed on!

Here's an example: Darren liked to go out to a popular dance club. One night, he struck up a conversation with a woman he found attractive and invited her back to his apartment. The woman agreed and went home with him. Once at his place, Darren took out his high school yearbook and a box of old photos. He spent the next two hours showing photos of him growing up. While Darren thought it was a nice way for the two of them to get to know each other, it was not at all what the woman was expecting. She left frustrated, and Darren was confused as to what went wrong.

Knowing what you now know about consent, you can see how taking an extra moment to clarify what was going to happen could have resulted in a better evening for both of them. They each thought they knew what the other wanted, but without checking in about those expectations, they had a disappointing encounter.

Here's another example: Claire was asked out on her first real date by a volunteer working the same black-tie charity auction as she was. Having never been on a date before, Claire relied on the images of dating she had seen in movies. When the suitor came to pick her up, she was presented with a motorcycle helmet and told to hop on the back of the bike. She was in a long dress and high heels. When she paused to ask what the rest of the date

---

DOUGLAS).

might entail, her suitor told her of a lavish plan to take her to Wendy's. Her date thought it would be fun to do something casual. Claire went back inside, changed her clothes, and hopped on.

In both examples, the relationships were brand new. As you get to know someone it gets easier to know what to expect. If your spouse of forty years asks if you want coffee, you probably have an idea of what type of coffee. If you are going to visit your parents for a weekend, you might already have some idea of what the guest room looks like and what the schedule for meals will be. Knowing those things in advance will help you make decisions.

There will always be times in a relationship where you need to ask more questions. If the person you've been dating for several years says they want to go to bed, you might still ask if they want to go to sleep or if they are looking for a sexy time. You might ask, "Are you wanting me to come too? What should I wear?" Taking the time to ask shows you care. It shows you want to protect your relationship by making sure you are on the same page.

Getting Informed Consent

Think about something you have agreed to without knowing the full situation. Perhaps it was the last time you picked up a chocolate chip cookie only to discover it was oatmeal raisin. Or perhaps you agreed to look after your neighbor's dog, only to find it was a two-month-old puppy who needed constant supervision and a substantial number of medications. Or maybe you've had an experience like Darren or Claire, where a date didn't go as planned.

Take a moment to write down the situation. Remember where you were and how it unfolded.

_____

_____

_____

Now try to remember your response. How did you feel when you understood the situation fully, and recognized it was not what you thought you were signing up for? Were you surprised? Angry? Disrespected?

_____

_____

_____

What questions might you have asked to have better understood the situation?

_____

_____

_____

_____

Think about the reverse, where you had information and the other person did not. Perhaps you were selling a car and neglected to inform the interested buyer of an accident. Perhaps you made a clothing return and were not forthcoming about having worn the item. Maybe you've said you had substantial experience doing something during an interview, but in truth only dabbled in it. Perhaps you built yourself up during a date or left something out to a potential partner in the hopes of impressing them.

What's a time you deliberately left out information that might have affected someone else's decision?

_____

_____

_____

How did you feel afterwards?

_____

_____

_____

What might you have done to make the situation better?

_____

_____

_____

Getting informed consent is important, but making sure you have all the information can be tricky.

Imagine you are going over to a new colleague's house for dinner. If you know you have specific food concerns or dietary needs, you would want to share that. If you are vegetarian or happen to have an allergy, for example, you might ask if there will be a non-meat option, or you might offer to bring a dish yourself. We do this in our daily lives all the time. In fact, we're pretty good at it! We know the things that are important to us, and we find ways to tell people.

Using day-to-day situations is a great way to practice giving and asking for information regarding consent. Because we are familiar with it, we only need to give it more attention to make it a consent practice. As mentioned in the last chapter, the more we do it, the better and easier it gets.

Think of an activity you did in the last week. Take a moment and list five questions you asked, or should have asked, before deciding to go through with that activity.

_____

_____

_____

_____

_____

It's important to think about how you can ask for more information. If it is a first date and they ask if you want to go back to their place after, you could offer, "I'd love to get to know you more first, and see if we're looking for the same things. How would you feel about stopping by the coffee shop next door and chatting about what we'd both like to do if we go back to your place?" Taking an extra moment to have a discussion about what both of you want could make all the difference. This is your chance to make sure you are receiving the information you need to make a decision.

Go back to your list. For each of the questions you wrote down, take a moment to write down a way to ask for clarification or more information.

_____

_____

_____

_____

_____

Having all of the pieces of the information you need can make a big difference. Let's imagine you are on a date, and you ask the person sitting across from you if they are interested in a long-term relationship. They say they want a long-term, deep connection. It might sound like a full answer. But, what if their idea of a long-term, committed relationship is an intense, soulful connection, where the two of you are separated by continents, as they spend eight months of the year traveling? What if they don't think to share that until the next time they're getting ready to leave town?

Now, going back to your list, look at each item once more, and think of what secondary questions you might ask to be sure you are receiving the most critical information.

_____

_____

_____

_____

_____

Before moving on, let's think about how to ensure you are *giving* the information needed for someone to make an informed choice. The more you know someone, the more you will begin to know what is important to them. Imagine your best friend, whom you have known since primary school, has a week off from work at the same time you do. It turns out your boss has a summer house and has agreed to let the two of you stay. The cottage does not have a working indoor bathroom, and you know this might ruin the trip for your friend. You would make sure to talk to them about this so they could make the best decision.

When first getting to know someone, that might be harder.

Take a look at this example: Conner was set up on a blind date with Garth. The two hit it off and went back to Conner's home. The pair had a great evening, and before having sex, took time to discuss STIs, relationship goals, and the types of activities both were wanting. In the morning as Garth was leaving, he noticed mail on the counter addressed to someone else. When he asked about the mail, Conner explained he was still legally married, but had been separated for several months. For Garth, this was a breach of trust, and he never saw Conner again.

It's impossible to guess every piece of information someone else may want to know. The more each person is aware and informed, the more confident they can be in their decision. The goal is for everyone to feel comfortable, safe, and able to make a good decision for themselves.

So how can you tell which information to share and which to wait on? Some of that will be a process of discovery. As you get to know someone, you will have a better understanding of their values and preferences. Until then, you need to ask questions about what matters most, or open-ended questions like, "Is there anything else you would like to know?"

Their return questions will help you know when you need to elaborate. If you mention you will be flying across the country to see a friend, you will probably follow it up by giving more information. If your partner asks questions about where you will be staying and how you know this friend, that is a good indication that more information would be appreciated.

Giving information is as much a way to protect you as the other person. The more confusion and lack of clear information, the greater the risk to you both.

Things That Impact Sharing Information

Even knowing you want to share information, there are times it might be difficult. There are a number of factors that can contribute to a lack of understanding.

Language

If you have ever traveled to a different country with only your high school language lessons, you can attest to the frustration of not being fully understood. Asking the baker for a specific type of bread might be next to impossible if you only know the word for "food." You can try to explain, with gestures or other words, but it is hard to get across what you are trying to say.

It can be just as hard to understand what the other person is trying to say. A limited vocabulary or a lack of understanding means it is difficult to get the information needed. This often leads to misunderstandings, frustration, and even a sense of being lost.

This comes up even with a shared language. Language is always evolving, and new meanings are applied to phrases all the time. When "Netflix and chill" became a popular term, radio hosts enjoyed asking politicians if they enjoyed "Netflix and chill with their wife." When the guest responded that they did, the hosts would snicker, having tricked the guest into talking about sex when the guest thought they were talking about watching TV.

It can seem people are consenting to the same activity, when in fact, there might be an unknown language barrier that is preventing them from fully understanding what is being asked. In the mid 1970's a song came out called Afternoon Delight. This song, which to many was a lovely tune about skyrockets in the summer, was to others, clearly about sex.

It is easy to make a mistake when you're sure you understand what someone is saying. People often find themselves in misunderstandings around "something that everyone knows." Where a piece of information is important or critical to getting a message across, it's always a good idea to clarify what you mean or ask if the other person understands. Just because you're using the same words, doesn't mean you're talking about the same thing.

Knowledge Base

The next issue that can impact sharing information is the working knowledge base of both parties. Your personal "knowledge base" is made up of everything you know about a particular subject or activity.

Let's look at this example: Penelope had moved to a new town, leaving her job at a large company to work for a small, family-owned company. After starting, she asked what everyone was doing for the long weekend. Several of her co-workers looked at her with confusion, and informed her that the company didn't give employees time off for holidays. She started to ask about sick time or vacation, only to find those weren't offered either. With her experience limited to working for large companies, Penelope was missing knowledge that might have helped her to ask different questions before taking a new job.

It can be hard to accurately guess our own knowledge base, let alone someone else's. Think back to our examples in medical consent. For those patients, coming from a background without medical training, it would be unrealistic to expect them to know what questions to ask next. There will always be things you "don't know that you don't know."

Dealing with a lack of knowledge is never easy. Sometimes it's a lack of knowledge about the person with whom you're interacting, and sometimes it's about the subject or interaction itself. Finding ways to ask more questions can help. It can also help to ask open-ended questions like, "What else do I need to know?" or, "I'm sure I'm missing something. What else can you tell me?"

Think about the last time you offered to make dinner for someone. Many of us fall into the trap of saying, "I'd love to make dinner for you." That's where the conversation ends. Most of the time this turns out okay, and no one is hurt or vexed. However, steps can be taken to ensure the best outcome. The conversation could instead go like this:

You: "I'd like to make dinner for you. What kinds of food do you like?"

Them: "I really like Italian food."

You: "Cool! I have a great eggplant parmesan recipe I could make."

Them: "I'm actually allergic to eggplant. Do you know how to make chicken parmesan?"

You: "Yes! I love to make chicken parmesan! Do you have any other food allergies I should know about?"

Them: "No, just eggplant."

You: "Great! How's next Thursday?"

The conversation is still simple and brief, but you get the information needed to make this a consensual situation all around. With enough communication, you build the knowledge and understanding you need.

Honesty

Honesty comes up often with informed consent. When a person lies or is dishonest, informed consent is not possible. Any decision made will be based on the wrong information. While you might not be 100% sure of another person's honesty, you can be sure of your own.

Being honest is one of the single best ways to protect everyone involved. No one wants to be accused of being dishonest or hear they wronged someone. Being honest from the start will help ensure trust and connection. When all parties are truthful, people make choices that are best for them and proceed with full understanding.

Long-term, successful relationships are built on honest, candid communication about what each person is wanting and willing to give. Being upfront about what you want and your boundaries gives your partner the chance to agree. It also gives them the chance to tell you up front if they can't (or are unwilling to) do something. You can then decide if you are ok with doing things the way they want to, or if you want to do something else instead.

Having a history of being honest with people helps to establish trust, which goes a long way towards building a consent culture where each person believes they will be heard and respected.

Openness

Along with honesty, openness (also called transparency or transparent communication) can be difficult to assess. Being open or transparent means sharing information willingly, and giving details freely. It means avoiding withholding information that would be important in helping the other person make an informed decision. It helps everyone feel more confident about the discussion and the information being shared.

Being open is about sharing relevant information without being asked. When you're sharing, you want the other person to have all the necessary or relevant information so they can make the best possible decision. In turn, you want people to be open with you.

As you get to know a person better, you begin to know if a person means things literally, like "Netflix and chill" actually meaning they are only interested in watching TV and relaxing with you (as opposed to the double-entendre meaning of that phrase, which is, "put on Netflix in the background while we have sex," that we talked about a few paragraphs ago). You also learn if they respond with openness when discussing more personal matters, or what level of using euphemisms helps that person feel most comfortable. Knowing these things will help you better assess where you need more information or clarity before you are able to consent.

While you may never be able to know exactly what someone else is thinking, you can become more aware of your own desires and the difficulties you have in sharing information. Practicing good information-sharing, and insisting other people do the same, will help you build trust, connection, and skill. This will help ensure everyone is able to consent with confidence.

The Impact of Deception

It would be nearly impossible to share everything that might affect someone's opinion. Each individual needs to supply as much information as might reasonably be assumed to influence a person's decision. Let's take a minute to look at what happens in the case of deception.

In 2010, a man was taken to trial in Israel in a matter related to consent. He had gone online and pretended to be a pilot in order to seem more attractive to women and get them into bed. In Israel, this is considered a desirable profession, and is something that would have influenced a woman's decision to be sexual. The man, after being discovered, was convicted in court for his actions.[12]

This isn't an isolated incident! In the United States, two states have legislation regarding what is called "rape by fraud": California and Tennessee.

On a different scale, misleading someone about the intent of an encounter can be harmful as well. If you know you are only looking for a relationship to last one evening, it would be unfair to mislead your date into believing you are interested in a long-term partnership. You would be withholding information vital to them having informed consent, and this could lead to harm.

Can you think of other examples that might alter someone's decision on whether or not they would be interested in dating?

_____

_____

_____

What if you are not forthcoming about other relationships? If you are on a date and the person does not ask if you have another partner, do you still have an obligation to disclose that information? It would be a reasonable expectation to assume that the missing information would substantially affect your date's decision to consent to a relationship.

The famous case of Marc Christian MacGinnis and Rock Hudson deals with the issue of informed consent in regards to STIs. In this case, the former movie star (Hudson) neglected to tell his partner (MacGinnis) of his HIV status. MacGinnis sued Hudson's estate and his secretary. The lawsuit argued that Hudson had known of his condition, but made the decision to not inform MacGinnis. The jury found in favor of MacGinnis and awarded him substantially more than was being asked. Over the years, MacGinnis has maintained his intention was "not to 'sleaze Rock. It was to say that if you have AIDS, you ought to tell your partner, whether you're a movie star or

---

[12] Bilsky, L. (2009). " 'Speaking Through The Mask': Israeli Arabs and the Changing Faces of Israeli Citizenship, " Middle East Law and Governance, 1, 2, 166-209.

a postman."[13] This landmark case did groundbreaking work to drive home the importance of fully disclosing information to partners.

Any intentional deception destroys trust. Along with the destruction of trust comes the weakening of the connection and destruction of relationships. The best things you can do are be honest, be open, and hold your boundaries with the people in your life.

How to Mitigate Information Risk

So far we have gone over the history of informed consent, why informed consent is important, how to give and receive information, potential pitfalls in obtaining informed consent, and the impacts of deception. It is natural to be thinking of the many ways you might be misled. The good news is that there are lots of ways to help protect yourself.

The best way is to have a conversation ahead of time to establish a common language base and make sure you are clear about the plan. This is true for a job, a date, a medical procedure, or a summer vacation. Talk about what activities you want to do and what they mean to you. Do you want to go for a hike? Is that a two mile hike around the lake with peanut butter sandwiches, or a ten mile hike up the face of a mountain?

Share what you are clear on and what you are unclear on. If you are new to something at work, talk to your boss or a trusted co-worker about your previous experience and what questions you still have. Being open about your experience will help the other person to better assess what questions they might have, or what information might be important to pass along.

Practice negotiation and communication skills in your everyday life. If you go to a coffee shop and are handed the wrong drink, say something. If you have a special request for your drink, use that as a chance to get comfortable talking about what you want. As this becomes easier, move on to harder situations. Maybe your roommate plays music too loud late at night. Work on talking about the volume, and collaborate on a schedule when their music won't interrupt your sleep.

Earlier you took some time to think about what your boundaries might be, and some follow-up questions to ask in certain situations. As you learn more about what boundaries are most important to you, explore those limits. Talk to people who have similar boundaries and ask what has worked for them. If there is something you are looking to explore, do research on it before jumping in.

Practicing these tips will help you to mitigate risk. You can't always control the actions of others, so it is essential to trust your instincts. If you aren't getting the information you need to feel confident making a decision, say no or walk away. As discussed in the last chapter, think in advance about how you will leave the situation if you are not comfortable consenting. Create a plan for if things go wrong and stick to it. Lastly, ask for help if you need it!

At the end of the day, we are all hoping to have a good experiences that leave everyone satisfied and happy. Whether it be surgery, a meal, walking your neighbor's dog, a first concert, or a first date, having everyone aware and informed of the situation will help foster trust and ensure safety.

By doing some self-reflection, you can decide what you want to share and what questions are essential. Once you know what's important, review the best time to ask and how to bring up those questions. Watch for any words or concepts that are unclear or hard to understand.

[13] Boyer, Edward J. and Garcia, Kenneth J. "Rock Hudson's Male Lover Is Awarded $14.5 Million." The Washington Post. February 16, 1989.

Consider what information you have that might be important to the other person. While it can be hard to know what everyone is looking for, take a step back to consider information that might affect their decision. Share honestly and openly with the other person. As long as you're comfortable, consider over-sharing a bit to make sure the other person has the information they need.

Informed consent is all about having enough information to make good decisions. By obtaining as much information as possible, it will be easier to make a decision you are happy about later: it will set you up for giving an honest yes, or setting a clear boundary.

Chapter 4: Agreement & Boundaries

Now that we've talked about what it means to have the capacity to give and receive consent, and how to know if you have enough information to give and receive consent, let's talk about the step of actually giving an answer. While it seems like this should be simple—you just say, "Yes," if you want to do something or, "No," if you don't—it can be trickier. This chapter is about the complexity of giving and receiving a true and honest answer.

The Basics: "Yes" or "No"

When was the last time you said, "Yes," to something? Not, "Ok," "Sure," "Whatever," or other off-hand answers, but a clear and direct, "Yes." Take a moment and think about it. What was the request? Was it easy or hard? Did you hesitate, or give an immediate answer?

How about the last time you said, "No," to something? Not, "Nah," "I don't think so," "Un-uh," or some other negative, but a clear and direct, "No." What was the request? Was it easy or hard? Did you hesitate, or give an immediate answer? Did you feel safe giving a direct no, or was there a feeling of risk?

The higher the stakes, the harder it is to give a direct answer. Where we perceive risk, either to ourselves or to the other person, we often hesitate. We might not answer at all, or we might give an answer with some degree of ambiguity to avoid harm, injury, or risk.

When it comes to consent, this causes problems. Ideally, when we ask someone for their consent we want a clear, enthusiastic, and unambiguous response, so we know how they honestly feel. On the other side, we want the person receiving our answer to know, without a doubt, if we're agreeing or not.

In situations where there is little risk or emotional content, we often give a clear response. Imagine you're ordering a cup of coffee and the server asks if they can put a lid on your to-go cup. You answer, "Yes, thank you," or "No, thank you." These are low-stakes answers, and therefore it's easier to be direct.

Take the example from our last chapter, where your boss asks if you're willing to work late. You might say, "Sure," if you want some overtime. However, you may say, "Sure," because you're worried about keeping your job. You might ask for more information, like, "How long do you need me to stay?" in order to make a more informed decision. You might try to bargain, "Can I start later tomorrow if I stay late tonight?" You might give an excuse. Few people will answer with a direct no because the stakes are higher.

Imagine someone is asking for sex. This is a high stakes, high emotion request. Sometimes you may want to say either yes or no. You might feel you should say yes or no depending on your shyness, or fear of how the other person might react. You might worry about what the other person will think of you, fear retaliation, or in some cases, worry about violence.

Whatever the reason, people often feel pressure around giving clear and direct answers. At the same time, depending on the request, there can be a lot of tension around receiving an answer. This complicates consent.

Ideally, when someone makes a request, you want to give an answer based solely on your wants, needs, boundaries, and circumstances. That answer should be as direct, clear, enthusiastic, and easy to understand as possible. You want to give an explicit agreement or set a clear boundary.

When you receive an answer to a request, you want to respond with understanding and validation. The other person does not owe an explanation for a particular answer. You might want one, but wanting it doesn't make it necessary. Instead, respond with understanding and appreciation.

Let's look at how to do that in more depth.

What Does it Mean to Say Yes?

Think of a request where you answered yes. It can be an actual request, or a request you wish someone had made. Pick something with emotional weight to it—something that took thought.

What was the request?

_____

_____

What factors led to you saying yes?

_____

_____

What concerns did you have in saying yes?

_____

_____

What was your response? Was it clear and direct, or ambiguous?

_____

_____

Did you feel the need to explain your answer?

_____

_____

Did you regret the answer later? If so, why?

_____

_____

When you affirm or agree to something another person is asking, you are saying you will do it to the best of your ability. More than that, you're saying you have the capacity to make the decision, enough information to make the choice, the will or desire to do it, and the capability to at least give it your best try.

Any agreements should, at a minimum, be explicit. This means the yes you give should be fully and clearly expressed, with nothing implied or left to interpretation. There are a lot of examples:

- o "Yes."
- o "Absolutely."
- o "Yes, I would like _____."
- o "I completely agree."
- o "I will do _____."

An explicit agreement tells the other person you are completely willing to do something. It doesn't say more than that. It doesn't communicate how much you do or don't want it. It says you considered the request, thought about what it means to you, and decided to do it for whatever reason makes the most sense to you.

Explicit agreement is the basis of consenting to a request or activity. When you give it, you are saying you agree to do the thing of your own free will based on your own reasons. You are saying, "Yes, I will do what you asked to the best of my understanding and ability."

Enthusiastic agreements are even better. The yes you give might include some statement of desire, passion, or excitement. It is not only an explicit statement of agreeing to the activity, but also one of wanting to engage in it. Examples include:

- o "Yes!"
- o "Hell yes."
- o "I would love that."
- o "OMG, yes!"

Adding a statement of enthusiasm tells the other person you want to be there with them. It expresses some of your internal process and level of desire. It helps to create more connection and reassurance between you and the other person.

Only give an enthusiastic yes if you actually feel desire and/or excitement about doing something. Showing enthusiasm doesn't mean there isn't room for other emotions too. Imagine standing in front of the roller coaster at your local fair. You've been thinking of trying it, when a friend asks you to go with them. You might give a shaky yes. While you can confirm that you explicitly want to do it, a part of you is still nervous. The yes you give is both enthusiastic and hesitant at the same time. We often feel both excited and reluctant about an activity. People and emotions are complicated.

While it's valid to give explicit agreement where there may be a lack of enthusiasm, it is often good to evaluate why you're agreeing to something you don't have enthusiasm for. A lack of desire or excitement is often a clue to rethink something. Where there is active fear or disgust, it's good to rethink whether you should agree at all.

At the Consent Academy, we say agreement should first be explicit, and ideally, enthusiastic. We want to be both clear in our choice and excited about our desire when giving an affirmative. Either one can show consent. Both together show consent, build connection, and help bring people closer together.

Any yes carries a lot of implied meaning. The more complicated the request, the more implied meaning exists. If a request is only asking one thing—"Can I hold the door for you?"—there is less chance of confusion or misunderstanding. Requests involving only one or two components and specific time limitations are more explicit. You're agreeing to just those few things.

A request like, "Can we go on vacation together?" has more room for confusion and misunderstanding, because it involves hundreds of different behaviors, and takes place over an extended period of time. Agreeing to the initial request, without further negotiation, implies agreement to the whole vacation. Where people have different concepts of what those behaviors are or should be, even informed consent can be broken.

The complexity increases for each person involved. Between any two people, there are differences in understanding, meaning, language, and concepts. This happens due to differences in perception, understanding of the concepts at play, culture, identity, and dozens of other factors. The more people involved, the greater the risk of differences that lead to confusion or misunderstanding.

The first piece of good news is that you can reduce confusion through proper information sharing and capacity regulation. Making sure you discuss what's going into your agreement means all people involved have a better chance of being on the same page. Greater communication allows for greater understanding and a better level of agreement. Understanding your own level of capacity and checking in with the other people involved about theirs also helps.

The second piece of good news is that we manage this complication all the time! Minor variations or confusions are often cleared up intuitively or unconsciously. When people act in good faith, they manage to navigate this complexity pretty well, either by communicating more or by reacting to problems with caring and compassion.

Imagine you're working at an office and someone brings in donuts. The employees descend on the box searching for their favorites. One of your coworkers notices a sad expression on your face as you're stuck on a call. They grab you a donut with sprinkles, and bring it over. Whether you decide to take the donut or not, the understanding and compassion helps you feel better about that coworker, and the office in general.

The last piece of good news is, if you find yourself in a position where you agreed to one thing, and the person you're with is doing something else, you can tell them to stop. You have every right to withdraw your consent at any time and for any reason. We'll talk about that in more detail later.

Agreeing to a request, either explicitly and/or enthusiastically, means you're agreeing to the whole request unless you state otherwise. This is why it's so important to understand what's being discussed. Be clear in your own mind about what you're agreeing to and be direct in your statement of agreement. It is just as important to be aware of this complexity and potential confusion so you can be understanding and gentle when someone is responding to a request you make.

Skill Building: Saying Yes

We have the opportunity to say yes many times during the course of our day. The next time you come across the opportunity, try one of the following:

- Pause after someone asks you for something, and think about whether you want to do it or not.
- Ask for clarification about some part of the request before answering.
- Give a simple, "Yes," with no qualifiers or explanations.
- Give an explicit, "Yes," where you also repeat the request and say you will do exactly that.
- Give an enthusiastic, "Yes!" Show your level of desire or excitement.

Start with lower emotional level or lower risk situations until you get comfortable. The more practice you have with different ways of saying yes, the easier it will be in more difficult situations.

What Does it Mean to Say No?

Think of a request you answered no to. It can be an actual request or a request you wish someone had made. Pick something with emotional weight to it—something that took thought.

What was the request?

_____

_____

What factors led to you saying no?

_____

_____

What concerns did you have in saying no?

_____

_____

What was your response? Was it clear and direct, or ambiguous?

_____

_____

Did you feel the need to explain your answer?

_____

_____

Did you regret the answer later? If so, why?

When we give a negative response or disagree to something another person is asking, we are saying we refuse to do or participate in that thing. We are setting and holding a boundary around something we aren't willing to do. We are withholding consent.

It's important to say no. Healthy relationships are based on our ability to hold boundaries; to say what we want and don't want. Saying no when someone else makes a request is how we tell other people what we don't want. They are able to use that information to build a framework for what's okay and what's not.

We're using the word "boundaries" a lot, so let's define:

- A boundary is a stated limit that says what you're not willing to do or what behaviors you're not willing to engage in.
- We use boundaries to define not only our behavior, but to define who we are as individuals. It helps people to understand who we are because the act of stating limits gives definition to our personality. I says, "I can want something different than what you want, and that's okay."
- "No" is the simplest of boundary statements. It says, "I'm not going to do that."

Saying the word, "No" (or using another negating word or phrase), says you're not consenting to what you understand a request to be. Your understanding could be different than the other person's intent. When this happens, you can only respond to what you understand the request to be. Where there is any confusion, it is always safer to answer, "No."

It's possible to say no to parts of a request. If you're disaffirming specific parts of a request, be specific: "No, I don't want to hug you, but I'm happy to have a conversation." You can also set conditional boundaries when saying no: "I'm not willing to go out for pizza tonight unless we go to the vegan place on the corner."

There are many ways to say no, and just like agreeing, your boundaries should be explicit. This means the no you give should be fully and clearly expressed, with nothing implied or left to interpretation. There are many explicit examples:

- "No."
- "No, thank you."
- "No way."
- "No, I don't want a quick hug."
- "I disagree."
- "I won't do that."

Ideally, boundaries should also be enthusiastic or emphatic. This could mean that the no you give includes some statement about your feelings. It is not only a boundary statement, but tells the other person that you feel strongly in some way about not wanting what's being offered. Examples include:

- o "No!"
- o "No way in hell."
- o "Thank you, but I really don't want that right now."
- o "I will never do that."

Adding a statement of enthusiasm or emphasis tells the other person you really don't want something. It expresses some of your internal process and level of desire. This clear statement of boundaries helps create connection and reassurance between you and the other person. It takes the guesswork out of what's okay and what's not okay, and builds trust. The person making the request feels comfortable they have not crossed a boundary, and the person receiving the request feels confident their boundaries and autonomy will be respected.

For many people, saying no is challenging. In American society, we condition people to avoid saying no, to avoid conflict, and to please others. This is especially true for those who were socialized as female when growing up.

A simple no is more difficult than it seems, especially in intense situations. To practice stating a boundary, start small. Start by practicing in low-intensity, low-stakes situations.

Where needed, give more information. We discussed informed consent in the previous chapter, and that concept goes a long way. Imagine someone asked you to empty the dishwasher. If you're unwilling or unable to meet that request, you can answer with more information:

- o "No. I have other things on my to-do list to get to first."
- o "I don't have time to empty the dishwasher. I'm going to the grocery store on my way home."
- o "My back is bothering me today. I'd rather do the shopping so I don't have to bend as much."
- o "I can empty the dishwasher if you go to the grocery store."

A request was made, a boundary was stated, and information was given making the boundary easier to understand.

When you are the person making the request, practice leaving space for the other person to give an honest answer. For example, instead of saying, "I'm going to the grocery store. It would be great if you could empty the dishwasher before I get home," you could say something like, "I was planning on going to the grocery store after work so I can make dinner. Will you empty the dishwasher before I get home?"

This gives context to the other person, and leaves room for them to withhold consent and state why they cannot grant your request. Framing a request as a question, and then honoring the answer you receive will help you behave more consensually. It will allow those around you to give honest answers and remain comfortable in your interactions.

When you hear someone say no or set a boundary, there are things you can do to make the situation more consensual. It's simpler than you might think. The best answer to someone saying no is, "Thanks. I appreciate you being honest with me!"

It's important to remember that someone saying no to your request is not about you. It's about them figuring out what they do or don't want and communicating that. People set boundaries for hundreds of different reasons. It's about creating safety and increasing communication.

This won't eliminate feelings if someone says no to something you want. Feeling disappointed or upset is normal. Always remember, it's not the other person's job to help you deal with or manage those feelings. Those are your feelings. They are your responsibility.

Avoid asking people to explain themselves if you don't like the answer. They don't owe you any explanation. Accept the answer and move on. If you want to know why they said no, you can make a new request, "Can I ask you why you don't want to _____?" The other person can then either consent to engage in that conversation, or set another boundary.

Boundaries are good and healthy things.

It is never okay to try to convince or force someone to change their mind when they have said no. Once a boundary is stated, consent has been withdrawn. Trying to push someone to change their mind is *coercion*.

Coercion is defined as "persuading someone to do something by using force or threats." Continuing to try to convince someone to say yes means you're using force.

If you find yourself in a situation where someone is being coercive or isn't hearing your no, walk away. Don't stay in a situation where a person isn't respecting your autonomy. Don't try to argue or convince them to listen to you. Just walk away.

Skill Building: Saying No

We have the opportunity to say no many times during the course of our day. Many people struggle with doing it clearly. The next time you have the opportunity to say no, try one of the following:

- o Pause after someone asks you for something and consider whether you want to do it or not.
- o Ask for clarification about part of the request before answering.
- o Give a simple, "No," with no qualifiers or explanations.
- o Give an explicit, "No," where you also repeat the other person's request and say you won't do that activity.
- o Give an enthusiastic or emphatic, "No!" Show your actual lack of desire or discomfort.

Start with lower emotional level or lower-risk situations until you get comfortable. The more practice you have with different ways of answering no, the easier it will be to do it in difficult situations.

What Does it Mean to Say Maybe?

Think of a request you answered neither yes nor no to. It can be an actual request or a request you wish someone had made. Pick something with emotional weight to it—something that took thought.

What was the request?

_____

_____

What factors led to you avoid saying yes?

_____

_____

What factors led to you avoid saying no?

_____

_____

What concerns did you have in giving a clear answer?

_____

_____

What was your response?

_____

_____

Did you regret the answer later? If so, why?

_____

_____

Did you wish you had given a different answer? If so, what?

_____

_____

As mentioned before, there are a lot of reasons you might not give a definitive yes or no. The most common is because you don't know what you want. Maybe the request is too complicated. Maybe you need to ask someone else first. Maybe you haven't had enough time to think about it. Maybe you're just not sure. Maybe you want to, but don't have enough time right then (or whenever the requested action is taking place).

Being unsure, for whatever reason, is okay. There's nothing that says you need to have an answer to something the moment it's asked. There's nothing to say you *ever* need to have an answer. You have every right to be unsure about something. How you answer when unsure is the important part.

When you tell someone maybe, you are stating, "I'm not saying no." You're letting them know you might say yes, but there is something holding you back. If that's what you mean, great! And it's better to be more explicit. Tell them what you would need to say yes. Example: "I'd like to go out with you, but it has to be Thursday night."

If that's not what you mean, be more clear. Here are some examples:

o "I don't know if I want to do that or not."

o "I'm feeling torn. Give me some time to consider it."

o "I don't have enough information. Please tell me more about _____."

o "I can't answer until I check with someone else."

o "I need more time to think about it. Give me _____ minutes/hours/days."

o "I can't answer that right now. I'll get back to you in _____."

o "I don't know. And I'm not sure how long it will take me to figure it out. Best assume the answer is no. I'll let you know if it changes."

There may be times when you can't say no, but don't want to say yes. This is hard. It sets you up for something called cognitive dissonance (the state of having inconsistent thoughts, beliefs, or attitudes, as related to behavioral decisions[14]). It also sets up stress and resentment. In other words, it reduces feelings of safety, lowers connection, and damages relationships.

Let's go back to our example of your boss asking you to stay longer to help with a project. When faced with this request, you might find yourself wanting both to stay and leave. You know that staying will please your boss and strengthen your reputation at work as someone who can be relied upon, which will help you come review time. You might also be thinking about how you were looking forward to going home early and watching an episode of your favorite show with your partner. In this example, both sets of thoughts and their related feelings would likely have you experiencing cognitive dissonance, recognizing both the advantages and sacrifices of saying yes, and the different advantages and sacrifices that come with saying no. This is a simple example and, provided you have an understanding boss, one that is fairly low-stakes. Not all times when you can't say no, but don't want to say yes are low-stakes, however.

When you find yourself in this situation, it can feel like there's no way out. You might feel angry, scared, or frozen, or think that you would do anything to get out of the situation. The best thing you can do is stay calm and be true to yourself.

Here are some things you can say:

o "Thank you for asking. Let me think about it."

o "I'm not sure. Let me get back to you."

o "That's a great question. I can't do that right now."

o "I can't say yes. I can't say no. This is really uncomfortable."

When someone tells you maybe, or some other statement that's neither clear agreement nor a clear boundary, it can be hard to know what to do. Where there is uncertainty, people tend towards the answer they most want or expect. This is an example of confirmation bias[15], and often leads to misunderstandings and hurt feelings. At worst, it can lead to a Consent Violation.

---

[14] Festinger, L. (1957). *A Theory of cognitive dissonance.* Stanford, CA: Stanford University Press.

[15] Heshmat, Shahram (2015, April) What is Confirmation Bias? *Psychology Today.* Retrieved from:

Always remember that unless you have an explicit and/or enthusiastic yes, you do not have consent. Where you are looking for consent for an activity or interaction with another person, any maybe or ambiguous statement should be taken as a lack of consent. This is neither a clear boundary nor a statement of clear consent. Therefore, you should not pursue the activity.

It is okay to ask for clarification. You can say something like:

- o "I'm not sure if that's a yes or a no. Can you be more clear?"
- o "If you need more time, that's ok."
- o "Just let me know when you have a definite answer."

It's always good to ask for clarification if you're confused, but only ask once. If the person isn't able or doesn't want to give an answer, once is enough to determine that. Asking repeatedly is coercive.

To help, you can reassure the other person it's okay to say no. People can find it hard to say no, or may feel stuck in some form of cognitive dissonance. You can say something like, "I want you to know I'm completely okay if you say no. I want you to be okay with anything we do before moving forward." This may give someone the space they need to set that boundary. Knowing their boundaries will be respected may help them feel safe enough to say yes.

Always respect other people's boundaries. Anything else is a violation of their consent.

The Danger of a "Coded Yes"

A *Coded Yes* is a term or phrase that gives the sense of agreement without communicating a clear yes. It's a way for someone to agree without using the actual word, and is common when someone feels they shouldn't agree to something even when they want to. This is an attempt to give consent without being explicit.

Some examples:

- o "Uh, okay."
- o "Ohhhh, that's great."
- o "That's hot (or yummy, or amazing, or any other word meant to convey goodness)."
- o "Mmmmm."
- o "What a good idea."

People use a Coded Yes for many different reasons. Sometimes they feel ashamed of what they want. Sometimes culture says the thing they want is wrong or bad. Sometimes they're afraid the other person will see them in a negative way. Sometimes they have uncertainty, and want a way out if things go poorly.

You can probably guess why using a Coded Yes is dangerous. Although a Coded Yes is giving consent, it is not explicit consent. Therefore, it carries an increased risk someone's consent will be violated.

If you find yourself using this type of phrase to give consent, take a step back and think about why. Do some extra work to understand what's preventing you from being clear. If you find you're using it because you don't want something, switch to practicing boundary setting. If you find you're having a hard time saying yes due to shame or cultural expectations, work on those feelings until you can be clear. If you need help, talk with friends or seek out a therapist.

https://www.psychologytoday.com/us/blog/science-choice/201504/what-is-confirmation-bias

If you find yourself receiving a Coded Yes, ask if you're willing to accept the risk of not having explicit consent. This will depend on the type of request, activity, and level of risk. If you do accept the risk, remember that you are then responsible for any misunderstanding or violation that happens. If you're not willing to accept the risk, ask for more clarity. You can say something like, "I want to do _____ with you. It looks like you want to do _____ with me. Is that true?"

Because a Coded Yes is something people use all the time, it's important to note that it's not wrong. When put together with nonverbal signals, a Coded Yes can show consent, but it always carries a higher level of risk.

Verbal vs. Nonverbal

People also use nonverbal signals to either show agreement or to set boundaries. Again, this happens for a lot of different reasons. Sometimes it's hard to say the words, "Yes," or, "No," out loud. The higher the level of emotion in a request or situation, the harder it can be to verbalize.

In western culture people often nod to express a yes and shake their head to express a no. It's something learned as toddlers. For some people, using nonverbal communication is easier. For others it feels safer or seems more appropriate. Sometimes it's necessary. Ever been to a loud concert or club where the only way to communicate is through head movement and hand gestures? That is one of many instances where nonverbal communication becomes critical.

It would be a book unto itself to describe all of the nonverbal signals and gestures used to show either agreement or boundary setting. There's a lot of subtlety and complexity. We understand many of these signals intuitively. We see them, and our brain interprets what they mean without conscious process.

This seemingly "automatic" understanding can make nonverbal cues extremely easy to misinterpret. Not only is there the danger of missing the cue entirely, there is also a greater chance the cue will be confused with something it's not. As mentioned before, where there is confusion, people are more likely to interpret what they're seeing as being in line with what they want.

Interpretation is hard even with active attention. Where there is reduced capacity due to substances, arousal, emotional concerns, fatigue, other physical concerns, etc., correct interpretation of nonverbal cues becomes even more difficult. Situational factors like lighting, distractions, and context further complicate things.

It's important to note that there are many people who are unable to recognize nonverbal cues. This is most often due to mental health conditions or traumatic brain injury. These folks may miss nonverbal cues entirely, or be unable to understand what they're seeing.

Knowing nonverbal cues are easy to misinterpret, confuse, or miss entirely makes it crucial to emphasize or confirm their meaning. If you're the person giving the cue, make it as direct and clear as possible. If someone asks you for a hug, and you want a hug, throw your arms wide open and step forward to show them. If you're the person receiving the cue, confirm your understanding before proceeding. If someone throws their arms wide ask them, "Hug?" and wait for confirmation.

Where there's any confusion, stop and switch to verbal, signed (sign language), or written communication. It may take longer, and feel a little awkward, but it will help you make sure your messages are being communicated and received accurately. When it comes to consent, you want to make sure you've reduced the possibility of confusion as much as possible.

Again, this is an issue of risk-mitigation. Using nonverbal cues is not wrong. They are an important part of communicating. When it comes to consent, relying solely on nonverbal cues creates higher risk. If you choose to engage in that risk, remember that you hold responsibility for what happens if something goes wrong.

Other Things that Increase Risk

Consent is not a clear black and white issue. It has a lot of complexity. The quantities of clarity, ambiguity, enthusiasm, and trust you have with the other person or people in the interaction can all be relevant in defining how much risk is involved in any given situation, regardless of the outcome. Think of it as a spectrum, with a low risk of confusion, misunderstanding, and Consent Violation at one end, and a high risk of those things at the other.

Here are some things that impact risk in agreement and boundary-setting statements:

- o **Level of Explicitness:** How clear and unambiguous the statement of either agreement or boundary-setting is. This can be determined by word choice, clarity of language, and/or the amount of explanation in the statement.
    - Low Risk statements are explicit, with a clear and direct expression of whether the request is being agreed to or not, and include clarification on any potential confusions.
    - High Risk statements are ambiguous, open to interpretation, and have no or little confirmation of what is being agreed to.
- o **Level of Specificity:** How direct and specific the agreement or boundary-setting response is. This can be determined by the verbal, nonverbal, and/or contextual communication that goes into the statement.
    - Low Risk statements are verbal or written with a high level of detail. They include matching nonverbal and contextual cues.
    - High Risk statements are nonverbal or contextual only. They are highly influenced by environment and capacity issues.
- o **Level of Enthusiasm:** How much the statement of agreement or boundary-setting shows the level of desire a person has. This can be determined by word choice, nonverbal expression, tone of voice, and/or the amount of detail given about internal process.
    - Low Risk statements have a high level of enthusiasm that is clear and easy to see. Verbal statements and nonverbal cues match or are congruent.
    - High Risk statements have little or no enthusiasm shown or perceived. Verbal statements and nonverbal cues are incongruent.
- o **Level of Perceived Trust:** How much trust the participants have in one another. This can be made up of a hundred different things, including personal history, level of connection, perception of how the person treats others, verbal and nonverbal cues, and/or many other things.
    - Low Risk happens where there is a high level of trust.
    - High Risk happens where this is a low level of trust.
- o **Level of Coercion:** How much an individual is attempting to achieve a specific answer. This can be determined by word choice, nonverbal cues, power differentials, previous history, expectations, and/or many other things.
    - Two primary types of coercion are asking a person to change their mind after they set a boundary, and badgering the person who's set the boundary with questions after they've given their answer.

- Low Risk statements happen where there is no coercion: where boundary statements are neither questioned nor pushed against.
- High Risk statements happen where one person attempts to force the other verbally, emotionally, or physically, to either preemptively secure a specific answer, or to change their answer after it's been made.

All of these come together to define how much risk of confusion, misunderstanding, and potential Consent Violation there is. Ideally we want all of our interactions to be low risk. Sometimes, due to the circumstances or people involved, you might find yourself in a higher-risk circumstance. That's okay. Remember, choosing to engage in a higher-risk interaction means dealing with any consequences. If you know what you're getting into, and feel comfortable with the perceived level of risk, you can plan around potential problems and work to reduce risk.

It can get a little overwhelming to process all the complexity, especially when you consider we often make decisions about giving or withholding consent in less than ten seconds. We often go with a "gut" instinct, and hope it all works out.

Most of the time it does work out, and we don't think about consent being involved. It's the times when it doesn't work and someone gets hurt that we tend to notice. The more significant the hurt, the more likely we are to examine what went into a Consent Incident.

To help illustrate how agreement and boundary setting can work, here is a quick story about Donna and Brin.

Story: Sleeping Together

Donna and Brin had been dating for three weeks. They met at a bus stop after both being stood up. They hit it off almost immediately, and started going out that very night.

The first few dates were focused on getting to know each other: holding hands, and sharing their favorite places. Donna took Brin to her favorite Indian restaurant, and Brin took Donna to her favorite ice cream place. They had a great time together.

On their fifth date, a quiet night on Brin's couch cuddled up with her cat and an 80's action movie, Donna leaned over during the credits, and (in a sultry voice) asked Brin if she could stay the night.

Brin pulled back, looking a little confused and tense.

Donna held up her hands. "Hey, it's cool if you're not there yet. I didn't mean to startle you. I felt really close and thought I would take the chance. No pressure either way."

Brin shook her head. "It's fine. Just give me a sec to think."

Donna waited. After a minute or so Brin leaned forward and took Donna's hand. "I'm not sure if you're asking me for sex, or if you want to sleep—like actually sleep—with me."

Donna smiled. "I was asking if you wanted to have sex. Guess I should have been more clear."

Leaning forward Brin whispered, "I would love to have sex with you tonight. There's a few things we should talk about first."

"Happy to," Donna replied kissing the other's ear.

"And, while I would love to have sex with you, I'm not ready for you to stay the night yet. I would need to work up to that."

Donna thought about it for a second, then said, "Okay. I would like to try sleeping too, and I'm okay to wait on that until you feel more comfortable."

"Great. So, just to check in…"

Practicing good consent in the agreement/boundary-setting phase is about being open, clear in your communication, and honest about what you want or don't want. If you can do that, most of the rest of the issues will work out. Where there is something more complicated or significant, take your time and answer with more care.

The Problem with a Coerced or Perceived Yes

We talked before about coercion and how to avoid doing it. It's worth talking about more. One of the issues we often deal with in our work at the Consent Academy is some form of the statement, "They said yes, so everything was fine."

Among some, there is the idea that if a person says yes in any form, however that yes is achieved, there are no issues of consent. It's the idea that getting a verbal yes makes everything that comes after consensual. This concept, beyond being overly simplistic, has significant issues.

People are too often forced into saying yes when they don't want something. This can be achieved through direct force or harm, the threat of force or harm, or the implied threat of force or harm. This force can be verbal, emotional, physical, or social.

The act of coercion itself is harmful and psychologically damaging. It takes away a person's autonomy and their ability to make decisions about their own body and mind. It damages connection and destroys trust. Done repeatedly, it can cause compounded trauma and a host of psychological problems.

Getting someone to say yes when they don't mean it is *not* consent. Badgering or threatening someone until they give in to what you want is bullying, at best—and probably more accurately categorized as assault. It is a violation of consent.

Avoiding coercive behavior is done by listening to and respecting what the other person says without argument or pressure. If someone says, "No," the appropriate answer is, "Okay." That's it. Additionally, you can use other skills—like clear communication, validation, emotional regulation, and self-awareness—to find your way to more consent-based interactions.

The "perceived yes" issue is summed up in the phrases, "I thought they said yes," or "It looked like a yes to me."

This goes back to the issue of confirmation bias: when someone *wants* the other person to say yes. They want it so much, they look for anything that even comes close to a yes—so even the smallest cue is taken as consent, while things that withdraw consent or set boundaries are ignored.

Thousands upon thousands of Consent Violations happen this way. One person perceives agreement where it isn't present. That person proceeds as though they have consent, when they don't. Consent is violated, and harm is done.

Then, after the harm is done, excuses are made:

- o "Well, they obviously wanted it."
- o "Their lips said no, but their body said yes."
- o "Did you see what they were wearing? They were asking for it."

This is not consent, and those are poor excuses for violating consent.

Avoiding this behaviour is about listening to what the other person says regardless of what you want. Your wants and needs are fine, as long as they stay in your body. When someone else says something you don't like or don't agree with, any feelings you have are yours to work through. The other person doesn't owe you anything.

Often coercive behavior and misperception of a yes happens out of ignorance, lack of skill, overwhelming emotion, and/or poor education. Rarely are these things done on purpose, with the intent of violating another person. However, whether it's on purpose or not, there is still a violation and harm done.

People can learn to do better. It's part of why we wrote this book. Learning to avoid these behaviors and use better consent requires three things: 1) Understanding what consent is, 2) Learning how to do it, and 3) Practice.

If you find yourself acting in a coercive way or engaging in confirmation bias, ask for help. If someone points out that you're doing either of these things, take them seriously and analyze how you're behaving. Getting help can include things like engaging in an accountability process, practicing consent in lower emotional situations, and sometimes working with a consultant or therapist to help change the problematic behaviors. It's not easy to change these things, and it can be done.

The most important thing is to recognize that the people around you have the innate right to say either yes or no to any request. They have the right to give their consent for a situation if they want to do it, and the right to withhold or withdraw that consent if they don't want to. They have the right to make decisions about what happens to their body, mind, and spirit. This is called autonomy, and that's what we're going to talk about next.

Chapter 5: Autonomy

Autonomy is the ability to say what happens with and to your body, mind, and spirit. When we use these three terms, we're referring to your physical person and bodily sensations as your "body," your thoughts or cognitive processes as your "mind," and your feelings or emotions as your "spirit." Autonomy is the freedom of choice for all of these parts of your "self" which are working in conjunction. This includes being able to choose how long something happens, free from external control or influence. It is an inherent right of all people, regardless of their appearance, age, relationship status, social standing, or any other identity or factor.

Autonomy is essential to understanding consent. Without personal autonomy, you may not recognize your right and ability to make choices—to give or withhold consent. Without the concept of autonomy, you may not recognize that others have the right and ability to make choices for themselves—to give or withhold their consent. In many ways, consent cannot function without the basic assumption of autonomy for all.

As you read this chapter, think about the concepts you've already encountered and how those elements, necessary for the practice of consent, are built on the idea of autonomy.

What is Autonomy?

In essence, autonomy is the right of every person to say yes to what they want, and no to what they don't; it is their ability to give or withhold consent. It encompasses the whole of our being: our body, our mind, and our spirit. And it applies to everyone, all the time.

When we are young, we have limited autonomy. We have limited ability to control where we go, or even what we eat. As we grow, our world expands and we gain independence and the ability to make our own choices. We learn information from our families and people who are close to us, from educational opportunities, and from our own experiences, all of which add to our list of choices. Think how dependent you were as a small child, and how that changed over time. What contributed to those changes? Were your own choices part of that change?

While you had some autonomy as a child, you had limited experience, power, and agency to enforce it. The more you learned, grew, and developed a sense of self, the more you were able to take control and assert your right to say what happened to that self. At the same time, you grew in your understanding that others were different and separate from you. You started to understand that they too had the ability and right to assert what happened to them.

And that's where things start getting complicated. If you and another person both have that right, what happens when there is conflict? If we're alone, autonomy is relatively easy. Where our choices intersect with another, autonomy helps us navigate consent, set boundaries, and have an awareness of both in others.

Let's look at some specifics.

Physical Autonomy

Physical autonomy encompasses the freedom to make choices about what *you* do with your body, and what happens to it (meaning what *other people* might do to or with it). It can mean anything from consenting to or rejecting a hug, to what fitness regimen or exercise you do, to where you sit in your house. This is also called "body autonomy" or "body sovereignty."

Physical autonomy is enshrined in our legal system, and at the same time is a right that can be removed as a punishment when someone commits a crime. We recognize that infringing on another person's physical autonomy is illegal: witness the laws around everything from kidnapping, to rape, to physical assault. A large proportion of our laws connect back to the concept that no adult is allowed to limit the physical autonomy of another adult without cause or consent.

This is not to say there aren't exceptions. People's physical autonomy is limited and imposed on every day. Some of these impositions are small and barely noticed, like laws that dictate wearing seat belts. Others are significant and can have a lasting impact, like repeated unwanted touch, reduction of freedom (external physical restraint), and other abuse.

Limitations or impositions can be done by mistake, or performed intentionally. The impact of the imposition on the person who experiences it varies based on many factors. For example, when an imposition on autonomy is seen as intentional, it often has a more significant emotional and mental impact, even if the actual physical impact would have been the same if it had been unintentional.

Imagine someone bumps into you. This is an imposition on your physical autonomy because you were touched without permission. The impact would depend on how hard you were bumped, where the contact occurred, and if you were hurt or injured by it. It would also depend on your perception of intent. If you see the bump as a mistake, you might think of it as "no big deal." If, however, you believe the person bumped into you intentionally, the impact is likely to be much more significant.

Let's look again at the example of hugging. When someone grabs you, without getting permission first, they are demonstrating a disregard for your physical autonomy. They are, in essence, communicating that their desire to give you a hug overrides any possible desire you might have to not be touched. They are saying their wants (and possibly their "self") are more important than yours (or you).

Many people experience fear or anger when this happens. It decreases their feelings of safety, both in general and with the individual who grabbed them. It damages any trust they had with that person, which will take effort to rebuild.

And this is a hug—something many of us do regularly. Imagine how much more significant the reaction is when a person's physical autonomy is compromised in other situations. Where there is sexual or intimate touch, the significance—and thus the impact—is much higher. The same is true when unwanted physical contact is repeated multiple times or for an extended period of time.

Think about previous experiences you've had around physical autonomy. Take a moment to write about a time your physical autonomy was respected.

_____

_____

_____

_____

_____

How did it feel?

_____

_____

How would it feel to have someone wait for your permission before hugging or touching you?

_____

_____

_____

Think about a previous experience and write about a time your physical autonomy was not respected.

_____

_____

_____

_____

How did it feel?

_____

_____

_____

How would it feel to have someone touch or grab you without permission?

_____

_____

_____

How was your feeling of safety different in these two examples?

_____

_____

_____

Physical autonomy connects to our sense of safety. Knowing someone sees you as a person, with the freedom to say what does or doesn't happen to your body, increases safety. It is one of the most basic ways we experience and practice consent. When someone affirms your physical autonomy, it builds trust and affirms your freedom to make choices about your own body.

By demonstrating to others that you recognize and respect their physical autonomy, you increase their sense of safety and trust in you. By respecting their boundaries, asking for permission, and accepting their yes or no, you are creating consent culture: You are changing the world.

Mental Autonomy

Now let's talk about thoughts: what you think, when you think it, how you think, and what judgements you make. Mental autonomy is a recognition of the differences between our thoughts and judgements, versus those of people around us. Just because we think something doesn't mean the people around us have the same understanding. Just because we have a belief doesn't mean that other people do, or should, believe the same.

Exercising control over someone's thoughts can be done in two different ways. First, someone can try to limit access to information. Examples include: telling you what books you can read, what television or movies to watch, what radio to listen to, what websites to visit, etc. These restrictions place limits on your thoughts and ability to gather information. Without exposure—or the ability to take in new information from a variety of sources—you diminish your capacity for giving informed consent.

Second, someone can punish the expression of specific ideas or ideas that differ from their own. Examples include: ridicule, dismissal of the idea, bullying, threats of violence, or telling someone they are wrong over and over. This causes people to question their thoughts and themselves. It is a diminishment of the person and their mental autonomy.

Both of these strategies are used in abusive relationships, by the media, by corporations, and even by governments. There is a long history of people trying to manipulate how others think as a way to control who they are and how they behave. We reject this. People have a right to think their own thoughts (remember, thoughts are different from behavior) and be their authentic selves.

How does it feel when someone tries to exercise control over what you think?

_____

_____

_____

What is a way you've encountered this?

_____

_____

_____

Part of how we acknowledge mental autonomy is through sharing our thoughts and encouraging others to share theirs. When we share thoughts and ideas, we get to know each other. This is another method for building trust and connection.

Sharing thoughts can cover a wide range of topics: everything from observations about the weather, to more vulnerable revelations about hopes and dreams. As you read these words, realize they are written by people trying to share their thoughts with you. Through this book, we are creating connections, safety, and trust... with you.

Respecting mental autonomy means you respect another's choice to share a thought with you, or to set a boundary around a particular thought. Demonstrating respect for both the vulnerability of sharing, and the need to set boundaries, creates greater safety for both of you. It deepens the trust and paves the way for sharing more intimate thoughts.

Recognizing when you are not ready to share a given thought, or don't wish to discuss a topic, also creates greater safety. When you communicate that recognition, it shows the conversation has limits, and gives you both a chance to demonstrate respect for each others' boundaries. It gives the opportunity to engage in consent.

Example: Amjeet was passed over for promotion. Upset and hurting, she goes into her boss's office to ask why. Her boss looks up as she comes in. Amjeet pauses, takes a deep breath and says, "I just found out I didn't get the project manager job. I know I'm qualified. Can we talk about what happened from your side?"

Her boss, after glancing at the calendar responds, "Yes, but I need an hour to finish a few things. I want to give you the attention you deserve and hear you out. Can we talk at 3:00?"

Amjeet is demonstrating trust, showing vulnerability, and signaling a willingness to wait until the conversation can be productive. Her boss is showing understanding, and a willingness to give their full attention. Both have demonstrated respect for each others' mental autonomy, and have built trust to help them through the difficult conversation. Both have contributed to building consent culture and enriching their working relationship.

Emotional Autonomy

Emotional autonomy is simple in statement, and complex in experience. You have the right to feel your feelings, independent of anyone else, their feelings, or what they think you should be feeling. Understanding emotional autonomy helps us recognize that the emotions we feel as individuals do not automatically match the emotions being experienced by others. If you or someone else tries to dictate how others should or shouldn't feel, you undermine their sense of emotional autonomy.

Couples and families often unintentionally violate emotional autonomy with little thought about the impact. We all have what we think is an appropriate emotion for a given situation. We then experience some degree of awkwardness or distress when we discover that someone we're close to feels differently. Sometimes, in that moment, we try to force our feelings on another.

One of the damaging things in many cultures is a persistent failure to recognize emotional autonomy. Whether due to our desire for independence or a need for control, there is a tendency to engage in self-referential thinking. That means we tend to see our perceptions and feelings as "correct," and believe others should see or feel things in the same way.

For example, if we love someone, we expect (or hope) that feeling will be reciprocated. But love is not transitive. Just because we love someone, we cannot force them to love us in return. The same is true of desire, fear, hate, or any other emotion.

We see this in parents and children quite often. The parent, with the learning and perspective of years of experience, can't understand why the child is reacting to something. The parent tries to change the child's feelings with statements like, "It's fine, you don't need to cry," or worse, "Don't you cry or I'll give you something to cry about." This is a denial of the child's emotional autonomy (and abuse via threats of harm, in the latter statement).

Think back on a time this has happened in your life. How did it feel to be told you were not allowed or not supposed to feel something?

_____

_____

_____

For most people, the denial of a feeling leads to stress and doubt. Some will attempt to suppress the emotion. This doesn't cause the emotion to vanish, but rather causes a build-up of emotional pressure. Others try to express the feeling even more, in an attempt to be heard or seen. This leads to a distortion of the original feeling, and often more misunderstanding.

Telling others what they are or aren't allowed to feel not only damages emotional autonomy, it also undermines a person's sense of safety and trust. This in turn causes people to lose touch with their own emotions, and reduces their willingness to share—which further diminishes the trust and caring between people.

Think about a time when you were growing up and felt safe to share your emotions, maybe with a family member, friend, teacher, or coach. How did it feel when that person validated your emotion? When they said, "Yes, I understand," or even, "Yes, I felt that way too."

How much were you willing to share with that person? How safe did you feel?

_____

_____

_____

What about a time when your emotions were invalidated: when someone told you a feeling wasn't correct, appropriate, or even okay? How much did you want to share with that person afterwards? How safe did you feel with them?

_____

_____

_____

Our emotions are a part of who we are. They are part of how we experience and react to the world around us. The more emotions we can name, and the stronger we feel things, the more we understand ourselves. Knowing we have the right to feel how we feel (remember, feelings and behaviors are different) helps us to both ask for what we want, and set boundaries around what we don't.

The more we are able to both respect and acknowledge the emotional autonomy of others, the more we build trust and understanding. When we're able to see and validate the feelings of others, we create a place for connection and consent to grow. In both these ways, we introduce space for consent culture to flourish.

How Does Autonomy Impact Consent

Let's look at how autonomy impacts consent. Imagine you live in a world where your right to self-govern, your ability to make choices about your body, mind, and spirit are unrecognized. It would impact everything from where you live, what you eat, who you marry, how you parent, and so on.

How do you imagine living this way would change your ability to move through the world?

_____

_____

_____

Throughout history, many people have lived in that exact manner and suffered because of it. The institution of slavery was driven by one group of people believing a different group did not have autonomy. Many of the oppressions faced by minority groups come down to not being seen as the same kind of person, with the same rights to autonomy, self-government, choices, and the right to consent.

Today we still deal with attitudes that declare one type of person as "more deserving" of rights and the ability to make choices. This is both wrong and dangerous. People often hold onto harmful ideas in order to feel better about themselves and have more control. Insecurity often drives people to exercise control over others instead of recognizing their sovereignty and working with them.

As we've seen in previous chapters, boundaries are a necessary part of consent. The ability to say no, to set a boundary, and to have that boundary be respected are all part of building trust. If you do not recognize that the other person has autonomy, you can't respect their boundaries. When someone sets a boundary, even one you disagree with, the best thing you can do is respect it.

When we recognize someone's autonomy, we are more likely to both offer consensual interactions and respect the responses we get. Because we see their inherent right to make decisions for themselves, we make requests instead of demands. We listen to the responses we get back and respect them, even when they differ from our own desires.

When someone recognizes our autonomy they do the same for us. When people make requests instead of demands, we take the time to answer truthfully and base our answer in our own desires. When people listen, we increase safety and connection.

How Does Consent Impact Autonomy

Autonomy is a necessary prerequisite for consent. If you're unable to recognize your own ability to make choices for yourself—to self-govern—then you're not able to give consent or set a meaningful boundary. You won't expect to be recognized by another, and won't expect them to respect your consent.

The more you practice consent, by saying yes to the things you want and setting/holding boundaries against the things you don't, the more you reinforce the strength of your autonomy. The same is true for listening to the yeses and nos of other people. Practicing consent creates a strong and deep recognition of autonomy, both in yourself and in others.

The daily practice of consent is key. Change comes from deepening our understanding and skill. Understanding autonomy is part of that change. It creates the freedom to be ourselves, to say yes or no by our own will, and to change our world.

Each boundary we make helps build the future we want to see, the life we want to live, and the respect we need to feel safe. Holding those boundaries is difficult. We all get tired, discouraged, and feel ready to give up when we see our autonomy thoughtlessly disrespected. When you practice consent, you create a safer world for yourself, your loved ones, and everyone. You demonstrate your autonomy and respect the autonomy of others.

Fostering Autonomy

So, how do you foster autonomy? How do you achieve a better world?

The first step is the hardest: Believe in your own autonomy. This starts with the recognition of yourself and your own rights. There are limitations and obstacles. We are still in the process of creating a better world. Believing in your right to govern yourself—to take actions and make choices rooted in what you want and don't want—is necessary to move in that direction.

The next step is taking action. Just one time today, give your consent or set a boundary based on what you want in that moment. It can be accepting the last cookie, or saying no to a hug you don't want. Whatever you try, be present in the moment. See how it feels to say yes or no, to exercise your autonomy.

Write down one way you can give consent or set a boundary today:

_____

_____

_____

_____

After you try this, notice how you are respecting other people's boundaries. Remember, respect for autonomy is a two-way street, and demonstrating respect for the boundaries of others helps increase trust. This, in turn, fuels the growth of consent culture in our world.

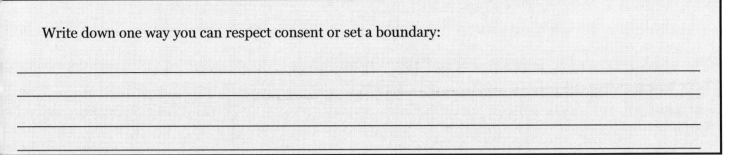

Write down one way you can respect consent or set a boundary:

_____

_____

_____

Consider a world where consent, respect, and autonomy can be the default for every person alive. Practicing autonomy every day moves us closer to that world, and we need your help. We cannot build a better world without you.

When Someone *Doesn't* Respect your Autonomy

There are people who don't use consent and don't respect autonomy. Sometimes this is intentional. Most of the time it happens due to misunderstandings, confusion, or emotional dysregulation. We want to help people change that behavior.

People who don't respect the autonomy of others are often deeply insecure. They feel their own autonomy isn't respected, is fragile, or is at risk of being taken away. These people haven't centered the practice of managing their own behavior in themselves. Instead, they see their behaviors as being centered in another: they believe that other people *cause* their own behaviors. For these individuals, observing someone exercising autonomy who is outside their sphere of influence (or more specifically, someone they can't control) can be seen as a threat.

Autonomy is rooted in an individual's authenticity and sense of self. It is based in their decision about what is right for them. It can be more difficult to practice when others don't see it the same way, but it doesn't remove the underlying truth: you get to choose what is best for you, even when someone disagrees.

When you encounter someone who doesn't respect your autonomy, you have a number of options:

o **Repeat yourself:** If your boundaries are not being respected, state your boundary again, using a clear and firm voice.

o **Walk away:** If you feel unsafe, leave. A person who does not respect your freedom to make choices is not someone you owe attention.

o **Ignore the person:** If you can't leave the situation, give your attention to someone or something else.

o **Ask for help:** Seek out someone who has more agency or power, and ask them for support or to stand near you.

o **Find like-minded community:** Reinforce your own autonomy by being around supportive and respectful people.

o **Learn better coping skills:** If you find yourself feeling scared or unable to enforce your autonomy, get help to learn better ways to enforce your right to make decisions for yourself. Therapists, coaches, and friends can all help.

By practicing consent, exercising your autonomy, and connecting with others who build trust and respect, you create consent culture. As it grows, more people will see the benefits. We are innately social creatures, and we take on the norms of the culture around us.

Even the most insecure and disrespectful people, if embedded in a culture that values autonomy and respect will start to change their views as they absorb what is happening around them. They may not like it at first, and may lash out, but over time they will start to adopt new ways of doing things. This is why we need you and your interest in consent.

By reading this far, you have a deeper understanding of consent, autonomy, and ways to help make our worl a better place. Keep yourself safe, practice with the people in your life, work on and talk about autonomy and boundaries. Once enough of us are practicing consent and showing how to respect autonomy, things will change Together, we will make a difference.

Chapter 6: Consent Frameworks

Now that you know the basic pillars of consent, we'll dive into consent within relationships.

How many times in a day do you have to stop and ask someone you know for consent, in the same way you would a stranger? We all have dozens of interactions on a daily basis. From the barista who makes your latte in the morning, to the person you sit next to on the bus, to your boss, co-workers, teachers, friends, parents, kids, the person you fall asleep next to (if you do), each of your relationships is different. For each of these connections we have intricate ways of knowing how to behave.

These ways of knowing are called consent frameworks. They are the sum of your knowledge about what a person likes/dislikes, wants/doesn't want, normally gives consent for, and normally sets boundaries around. Consent frameworks include both your normal pattern of behavior, and the understanding you use to make decisions about how to behave. Much of this happens on an unconscious level.

In this chapter we'll show you different consent frameworks and talk about how frameworks are built, how they're maintained, and how they evolve over time. We will also look at ways to keep your relationships healthy and flourishing through better consent practices.

Consent Frameworks in Public

How did you first learn how to behave in public? Was it a memorable experience? Did an authority figure, like a teacher or your parent, comment on something you did and show or tell you, "We don't behave that way?"

It's unlikely you learned how to "behave in public" through formal study—unless you travel, have been to finishing school, or have taken classes to learn about specific customs. Learning about what to do and not to do in public is something we do through trial and error, watching others, and mimicking behavior.

We learn in every new environment we encounter, and with every person we meet. We then build a consent framework around expected behaviors, the pieces of which are gathered from those interactions. This learning process is something most people do instinctively, and build into a model of what is appropriate behavior.

Regardless of where we are from, we all grew up with a set of "rules" for how we are expected to behave. When we're in a public place, such as a park or grocery store, we're exposed to the people in that area. We're exposed to their influence, and they're exposed to us. Our "rules" tell us how to behave and what behavior to expect from others.

There are many layers. We have people who teach us unspoken social rules, such as what is considered normal in a public place within a given culture. Friends, peers, parents, teachers, and bosses all help us build consent frameworks by instructing us in the unregulated rules of engagement. This can be advice on the order to greet clients when going into an important meeting, how to thank the host of a party, or when it's appropriate to hug someone.

Learning frameworks for a new culture or community can be complex. For example, remember or imagine the first time you went to a new church. Each religion, sect, and community has its own ways of worship. If you were not familiar with that particular community, things may have been confusing. You would have watched what other people did to see what was okay.

In the same way, how you greet someone is dependant on where you are and what your relationship is. There are places where a kiss on the cheek or a strong hug is a common greeting. In some places it is normal to bow or shake hands. In other cultures it is considered taboo to touch or even look someone in the eyes on a first meeting.

These public consent frameworks are something you learn by watching and seeing how others behave. When we enter a different culture or community, for most people, it creates a feeling of discomfort. People behave in unfamiliar ways, so we try to pick up on the "rules" of behavior. Once you become familiar with the basics, you begin to relax.

Outside of public spaces, we encounter institutional consent frameworks. These frameworks are built on policies, such as mass transit rider rules, student handbooks, or workplace codes of conduct. These are spelled out in writing, conveyed in training, and are enforceable. If you do not consent to the rules of engagement, your participation can be limited or terminated.

Consent frameworks, spelled out in this manner, have a limited range and may be confined to specific situations or locations. Once you leave the space, they no longer apply. These may require some type of affiliation, such as employment, or belonging to a club. Finally, there is oversight by an authority figure or governing body, like the Dean, Transit Police, human resources, or a board of directors.

We also have laws instituted by cities, states, provinces and countries. In the United States we have many such laws, passed by cities or states, to govern behavior. One example would be indecent exposure laws passed to deter people from exposing genitals in public. If someone does, they can be charged with a crime. Laws are society's way of saying, "That's not how we behave."

And, like many other things, it's complicated. How do we define what is right for the general public? How do we decide what is personal freedom and what impinges on the freedom of others? As an example, there has been a lot of debate over when and where the female nipple can be exposed in public.

Breastfeeding in public is now legal in all 50 states as of 2018, but that has not stopped wide-scale debate about the "naked" breast. In some places, women retain the right to go topless in situations where it is deemed appropriate for men to be topless. This debate has spilled over to social media platforms, where some have made attempts to censor the nipple as a sexualized body part. On some popular social media sites, users can be placed in a "timeout" for posting the unedited female breast.

Many women and gender non-conforming people are no longer consenting to their bodies being sexualized, shamed, or further censored. They are not adhering to the framework placed upon them through shame or domination. This type of social change is inevitable. By focusing on consent as a basis for that change, we can reduce harm and build better frameworks.

Frameworks that do not center on consent hold many people back from living their fullest lives. The negative ramifications that result from these non-consensual frameworks prevent us from expressing our true selves. It affects every aspect of our lives: how we talk, how we express ourselves, how we engage in relationships, our gender identity, our sexual expression, even how we dress.

Story: Imposed Stockings

When Lucy was a child, she had a drawer full of black and white stockings. Black were for winter and white were for summer. Her mother was raised to believe it was a sign of disrespect for young girls to go bare-legged. She was required, regardless of how sweltering the weather, to wear those leg-prisons every Sunday.

Her attempts to stage a jailbreak always failed. If Lucy tore her stocking and claimed she couldn't possibly wear something so ratty, her mother would magically produce a backup pair, breaking the five-year-old's heart. Arguing was pointless.

Mom grew up wearing stockings in public every day. It was what she had been taught by her mother as being proper and respectable. Bare legs were only for climbing trees and bike rides. Lucy being forced into restrictive, hot, twisted, and ill-fitting tights every Sunday was her mother's concession to the cultural ideal.

As Lucy grew up, she and her mom continued to argue about the stockings. It stayed a point of contention for many years, until, as a teenager, Lucy declared she wouldn't wear them anymore—and added, "You can't make me."

Years later, as an adult, Lucy would choose to put them back on, sometimes for style and sometimes for propriety. Given the choice, she found she could choose to wear them and be happy doing so. When she did, she would often think back to her mom and grandmother, both with nostalgia and regret that they didn't have the same option.

The dynamic between Lucy and her mother shows how frameworks can be passed down. The mother, influenced by unspoken societal expectations, created a framework of appropriate attire. She didn't ask her daughter what she wanted. She didn't give her daughter agency to make the choice for herself. Instead, the mother enforced her own concept of proper attire. This not only taught Lucy how to behave within a pre-established framework, it also had the unintentional side-effect of teaching that personal consent was less important than the social and institutional frameworks.

The expectation of stockings has evolved along with fashion and social understanding of women's power and agency over time. Currently, the wearing of stockings is a choice, not a requirement for social acceptance. Culture has changed, and women are granted more freedom in self-expression. Frameworks evolve and change, much like stockings.

This is an ongoing process. Evolutions in proper attire and societal expectations are constantly challenged. The shifts that happen involve hundreds of factors, ultimately resulting in a new framework which is then passed down to a new generation.

Story: Out for Coffee

Sara recently moved to a new neighborhood. During the grand unpacking, she found herself needing a break, so she jammed a ballcap on and headed out to find a coffee shop. The nearest place was bright and cheerful, with a punky-tattooed barista behind the counter.

"Good morning! I'm Rio, what can we get started for you?"

"I haven't been here before. I just moved in."

Rio began to chatter about their coffee and where it came from. They told Sara about the sizes and milk options. Sara ordered her usual: a soy hazelnut latte with light foam. Rio made it well, and Sara left happy.

The next day, Sara went back. Walking through the door, she was greeted by name. "You want your usual?"

Sara smiled, "Absolutely!" and felt like she was home.

The consent framework built between Sara and Rio was a brief encounter in public, for a specific purpose. Capacity on both sides was established through simple conversation. The barista made sure they were using understandable terms and vocabulary, and shared information about the available choices. Clear agreement is given: the customer pays, and the barista delivers the goods.

When Sara comes in again, the barista uses the knowledge gained the previous day to establish a growing framework: Sara's capacity, level of understanding, and history of paying. That framework was then put into shorthand, "You want your usual?" by which the barista was asking if the information and consent established in the last interaction held true in this one. Sara gave an enthusiastic yes, and felt a sense of connection, because she had been seen and her consent was acknowledged.

Not all encounters in public go smoothly. Every day your consent is both honored and disregarded. Sometimes it is flat-out violated. Remember, when you expand your idea of consent, you can see all the interactions involving it. You get to decide what you are willing to accept or reject in your interactions with others.

So how do you strengthen your personal consent framework? Good news: you have lots of opportunities. Imagine boarding a crowded bus at rush hour. You want to sit down after a long day and listen to your favorite podcast. You see an open spot and ask the person next to it, "Is this seat taken?" They gently shake their head no so you smile and sit down.

This is an example of building a framework of consent with a stranger, for a specific interaction and for a limited time. You had a desire, made a request, and respected the answer to that request by waiting for an honest response. You built, in a limited way, connection and trust.

The interaction continues. Your seatmate asks, "How was your day?" This might start an internal dialogue: "Should I engage in conversation, or keep to myself?"

Imagine you decide to keep to yourself. You reply, "You know, the usual," and slip in your earbuds. You do not make further eye contact, signaling you want to be left alone.

If your seatmate has good capacity, can understand your non-verbal cues, has the same cultural norms for when to disengage from conversation, and respects your autonomy, they will disengage. Your nonverbal statement will have been respected.

However, if your seatmate doesn't have the capacity or willingness to recognize your non-verbal cues, they may continue to engage. This might cause an emotional reaction—uncomfortable at best, and scary at worst. At this point it would be worth considering:

- Does your seatmate understand the cues you are sending?
- Were you clear in your statements?
- Does their behavior feel unsafe?
- What are your boundaries?
- Will you move seats, stand, or draw a verbal boundary if they continue to talk?
- Are there other factors involved, such as age, race, sex, or gender?

Imagining scenarios like this one helps you be prepared. Knowing your own consent framework when you encounter a situation like this helps make interactions smoother. Defining your personal boundaries, knowing what you are willing to consent to, and practicing saying no when you're *not* in a high pressure situation will help.

Skill Building: Consent Boundaries

Maintaining your own boundaries while dealing with other people is part of your personal consent framework. It takes time and practice, but the payoff is huge! It will serve you well when navigating both public situations and any other relationship. Below are some things to practice.

Creating a Personal Consent Framework:

1. Identify your limits: physical, mental, emotional, sexual, and spiritual. Write them down.
2. Be direct and clear. Some people, especially if they are a stranger, do not know how to read your social and nonverbal cues.
3. Give yourself permission to have boundaries. Practice saying what you need and want. Practice saying, "No." Give yourself permission to walk away if necessary.
4. Evaluate your reactions. We all have past experiences that inform how we live. Examining why you react the way you do can help you decide if and when to try a different way.
5. Ask for support. Talking to a trusted friend, therapist, or coach can help you clarify your thoughts and make sense of what you want to include in your framework.

Start slowly. Building a conscious consent framework takes time. Celebrate your successes, and take good care of yourself in the process.

Consent with Doctors, Teachers, and Other Professionals

The term "professional relationship" has a wide scope of meaning. In the strictest sense, it is a relationship governed by laws and/or guidelines. There are many different types.

One example is the professional relationship between healthcare practitioners and patients. In this relationship, a consent framework is based on laws and codes of ethics. Because of the power dynamics (you being ill, and your potential lack of medical training), capacity is lower and your risk is increased. To address that risk, there is enforcement and medical oversight to hold healthcare professionals accountable for implementing informed consent.

Another type of relationship that is governed by guidelines is the academic relationship between students and instructors. In grade school, where the age of the students decreases their capacity, teachers have more oversight with regard to behavior and class content. The student-instructor dynamic changes in higher education as students increase in agency. In continuing education, instructors come with varied backgrounds and oversight depending on the type of educator they are. The way adult educators conduct themselves varies depending on professional affiliations, institutional policies, and personal ethics.

Regardless of how regulated the interaction, it is important to be aware that professional relationships create a power differential. Typically, the person with the higher professional standing has the greater power. This creates a reduction in consent capacity, and may impact the ability to give full or autonomous consent.

Skill Building: Being Your Own Advocate

Think about different professional relationships in your life. Make a list of professionals you interact with on a regular basis: doctor, yoga instructor, teacher, therapist, etc. Rate your comfort level with questioning their authority on a scale of 1 to 10, with 1 being highly uncomfortable and 10 being perfectly comfortable.

Name   Profession   Rating

_____

_____

_____

_____

_____

Were there any surprises? If so, why?

_____

_____

If you were confronted with a recommendation you didn't agree with, what would you say in response?

_____

_____

Would you stay silent, or would you engage in further information-gathering or negotiation?

_____

_____

If it was difficult to think about speaking up for yourself, where did you most feel it in your body?

_____

_____

Are there past experiences, negative or positive, that inform how you interact in your professional relationships?

_____

_____

Do you need support in creating a personal consent framework surrounding professional relationships?

Who can support you?

_____

_____

What are some things you can do to make it easier to advocate for yourself?

_____

_____

_____

A Special Note to Professionals: Be a Consent Hero!

If you are a lawyer, healthcare professional, educator, or hold any professional position, we invite you to think about this exercise from your clients' perspective and consider the following:

o How would you rate?

o Are you engaging?

o Do you make a safe space to have open discussions?

o Do you present feedback to help establish boundaries?

o Do you invite questions?

o Do you make sure your clients understand options, procedures, policies, responsibilities, and jargon?

o Do you ask your client's consent before touching or interacting with them?

o Do you make space for regular check-ins and the ability for your client to say no at any time?

Consider your consent practices, and the positive impact you can have by developing a robust and aware framework. Make the first move and be a Consent Hero!

Consent in the Workplace

Relationships in the workplace are varied; they depend on the type of work, company culture, number of co-workers, expected level of productivity, and pacing. A busy catering company (where people are moving through their work quickly, and there are often many people in a limited space) is going to have a different feel than an internet securities firm (where people may work from home and have limited interactions). As you read this section, think about the jobs you've had and what those situations were like.

Large corporations often have employee oversight through hierarchical structures, including managers and Human Resources departments. These frameworks are established through written policies and procedures, and structured training. Smaller businesses tend to have less clear policies, as they have limited resources and fewer relationships to manage.

In all cases, there are consensual interactions not covered by company policy which may have a significant impact on your day-to-day life in the workplace. From casual interactions around the water cooler, to more formal interactions around the meeting table, there are lots of opportunities for consent. The relationships we have with our coworkers, as well as the consent frameworks we build, have a significant impact on our work satisfaction and perception of the company.

Workplace culture—and more directly, how people interact with each other—can have a big effect on productivity. If the culture is rigid and competitive, it is unlikely that employees will be flexible and open with one another. This may discourage partnerships, slowing down productivity, and push employees to avoid personal connection. Conversely, fostering a culture of curiosity and discovery helps encourage productivity through connection and the building of trust.

For example, if you have open communication with your direct manager, it will be easier to approach them with a question or concern. You learn the way your boss likes to be approached, even though that information is not covered in any training manual. Your ability to approach your boss can have a huge impact on your success at work.

If there is a consent situation where your boss is directly involved, unwilling to help, or if you're unable to go to them directly, it helps to have a network or policy in place. Knowing that information gives you options and increased agency.

The same goes for your co-workers, teammates, or mentors. We gravitate towards people we relate to, learning their work styles and accommodating their preferences. Some people may have a similar work-ethic or skill-set, and you can accomplish more when you work in tandem. Others may support you on a personal or emotional level, especially if you have similar interests or senses of humor.

Work relationships contain a blend of the professional and the personal, which can create blurry boundaries. It's important to be aware of how the power dynamics involved impact your ability to give and receive consent, as well as how your personal relationships may challenge your ability to give a clear agreement or state a firm boundary. Being solid in your own personal consent framework will help.

Story: Give Me a Minute

Juan once worked for a small, family-owned company, where there was no HR department. The culture was open, and everyone got along like one big family. Juan enjoyed the work, the culture of cooperation, and his fellow coworkers.

The only issue he had was the constant interruptions throughout the day. There was seldom an emergency, or even a time-sensitive issue, but the persistent distractions took him out of his creative head space. Sometimes he would need hours to pick up where he left off.

Juan was left feeling frustrated and annoyed with his co-workers. He tried holding up a finger as a sign of, "give me a minute," to nonverbally convey he wasn't in a space to answer a question, but his coworkers said they were offended. The more Juan tried, the more aggravating the situation became.

In evaluating the situation, Juan realized he was doing the same thing: he was approaching with no warning and demanding attention. It was apparent that this behavior was tied to the consent framework established by the company culture.

In an attempt to change, Juan decided to alter his approach. Instead of walking up to a coworker when he had a question or idea, he would jot it down. Later he would ask, "Hey, I don't want to interrupt your flow. Do you have space for a quick question?" Then, he would wait for an answer, respecting their autonomy.

Sometimes the answer would be yes, or sometimes they would ask for a few minutes. Juan thanked them cheerfully and told his co-workers he would be at his desk when they had a moment. It didn't take long before the office mimicked his behavior. It felt good and respectful. Their interactions were more focused and they got more done.

By evaluating the situation and trying a different approach, the coworkers respected each other's consent. They listened to one another and asked before interrupting. Being consistent and respectful, they were able to change the culture of their workplace for the better. Not only did it end up feeling emotionally better, they became more efficient.

Modeling how you want to be treated can be a powerful tool in establishing the consent framework you want.

Taking a step back from the situation and seeing your role in the scenario can be a daunting task. It can also be a powerful tool for change. Not every person—or workplace—is healthy and willing to make a change, but it is worth the effort to try. Consistency is key.

Skill Building: Modeling Consent in the Workplace

Sometimes it can be difficult to get people to honor your consent in the workplace. One way you can make change happen is to model good consent practices.

Modeling a Personal Consent Framework in the Workplace:
- **Know your values and personal limits.** Understand how they fit into the responsibilities and expectations for your job. It can help to write them down and post them where you can see them. If you know you have a limit on which days you can work overtime, having a reminder up helps you to hold your limit, and helps your boss to remember this is something the two of you had previously discussed.
- **Be consistent in your words and actions.** When you promise to do something with your words, follow through with your actions. Ex: "I can work late and do closing on Friday." Then make sure you are there and covering the closing process on Friday.
- **Avoid taking things personally.** If you notice that a co-worker seems upset, don't assume their upset is connected to you or your actions without them explicitly saying so. By doing this, you are demonstrating respect for your co-workers' autonomy and ability to speak up for their own boundaries and needs. You are also demonstrating that you know your co-worker can manage their own emotions.
- **Create structure for yourself.** If you know your attention is prone to wander at certain times of the day, such as after lunch, set up reminders to help keep you on-task. Make smaller goals when doing repetitive tasks to help you stay engaged, and reward yourself for meeting those goals. Consider establishing a daily schedule that puts more difficult tasks earlier in the day, or whenever you find yourself best able to concentrate.
- **Be willing to verbalize boundaries or limits with no guilt.** This is the parallel to "not

taking things personally" above. By modeling your willingness to state your boundaries and limits, you demonstrate the respect you have for your own autonomy.

- o **Have a plan for if your boundaries are broken.** Be willing to address violations in a timely manner. It's ok to take the time you need, but knowing what steps need to be taken can help you get past the "freeze" reaction we experience when our boundaries are broken.
- o **Take good care of your personal needs.** Make sure you have snacks at your desk and are taking regular bathroom breaks. Take time for your self-care if you feel yourself getting upset.
- o **Ask for consent when engaging with coworkers, teammates and managers.**
  - "Is this a good time to discuss this?"
  - "Do you have the bandwidth to answer this question now, or can we set a time later today/in the future?"
- o **Respect other people's time.** This can mean anything from showing up on time to meetings, to asking a co-worker what limitations they have during their afternoons for scheduling lunches, to asking a manager for a full ten-minutes instead of just saying, "Do you have a minute?"
- o **Show gratitude and celebrate when someone shows respect for your consent framework and boundaries.** For example, "Thank you for giving me an authentic answer," if someone tells you no.

Building a culture of consent will take time. Start with people you enjoy a good working relationship with, explaining to them what you are trying to accomplish. Model the behavior you want to see in others. Remember, your consent framework is important and worth the effort. Celebrate your successes, and take good care of yourself in the process.

Consent Frameworks in Intimate Relationships

The concept of intimate relationships, and how we define them, is unique to each of us. Most people consider relationships between friends, partners, and family as having some degree of emotional intimacy. These relationships are built over time through emotional bonds and personal interactions. They are strengthened through shared experiences and perspectives.

Over time, your relationships evolve, adjusting to new phases in life. Transformative events, such as puberty, leaving home, changing careers, marriage, divorce, and many others, impact the way you and the ones you love interact.

When moving through life, approaching each other with a spirit of respect is critical. To fully benefit from and enjoy intimate relationships, it's important to be open and receptive to new information. At times, we may need to make adjustments to our consent frameworks as relationships develop. The friend from college that would go out bar-hopping four nights a week might need to change his relationships now that he has a new baby in the house, or is moving back in to help care for an aging parent.

Luckily, as we age, our capacity for consent changes. When we learn more about ourselves and the world around us, our ability to understand and give informed consent grows. Our skill at giving clear agreements and setting clear boundaries improves. As we go through our lives, we develop a better sense of our own needs and desires, and learn how best to ask for those.

All of the skills and concepts we've talked about before go into maintaining a healthy intimate relationship. By being aware of consent and its concepts and ideas, and by practicing it as much as possible, you strengthen those relationships and provide opportunities for even greater depth. By understanding the framework you build with each of your friends, family, lovers, and/or partners, you have the opportunity to see the growth, change, and beauty within them.

While consent in our intimate relationships has the same basis as any other relationship, we have more opportunities to work and practice with the people in our closest circles. It is often easier to ask questions, get feedback, and make mistakes in closer potentially and more trusting relationships. The frameworks we build are normally stronger, more resilient, and more detailed than those we build with strangers or colleagues. We get more information, and we give more in return.

Keeping open communication is necessary and healthy when encountering change. Conveying information is one aspect. You have a responsibility to speak up when something in you changes, trying to be as clear and concise as possible. If you have just returned from dialysis with an ailing parent, you might need to set a new boundary and ask your friend from college to not call or text on Tuesdays at that specific time. Since this is a new boundary, it might require patience from both of you to remember. It takes time and work to maintain a relationship, but it's time well spent.

We've just been discussing close and intimate relationships, but you might be wondering why we haven't addressed sexual intimacy yet. Sex and sexual relationships are a topic all on their own, and we'll talk more about consent as it applies to sexuality in Chapter Seven.

Maintaining Consent Frameworks

Many people will learn someone's preferences, like a favorite meal, and assume that information will never change. For example, your best friend may have always loved a good steak, but now has suddenly become vegan. They forget to tell you, and you invite them to a 4th of July barbeque. The friend is unable to find anything to eat besides watermelon, and is clearly a bit annoyed.

How would you react? Would you be offended or angry? Why or why not?

_____

_____

How would you handle the situation?

_____

_____

Did you violate that friend's consent?

_____

_____

Some might say consent was violated, because you didn't ask, relying on prior information to inform your decision. This is where consent in long-term or on-going relationships becomes nuanced. People argue the need to ask for explicit and enthusiastic consent every time, with every interaction—which can be exhausting and, in many cases, impossible.

We build consent frameworks, not only to save time, but to build trust. When you honor someone's boundaries it shows respect and attentiveness. Even attention to the small desires and preferences of the people you love or care about creates intimacy, like remembering your friend loves cream sauce.

When changes occur and you are not aware of the shift, you are not automatically committing a Consent Violation, you simply need to check in. The information in your consent framework needs updating. Any error or mistake you make can be simply that: a mistake. The relationship, when strong, has the ability to weather mistakes.

If, however, you receive new information and react poorly—like being angry that your friend has decided to give up meat, calling them by the wrong name, or touching them in ways they've told you not to—you erode trust and violate consent. You signal an inability to adapt, and therefore you become less safe. In effect, you are telling your friend that your concept of them is more important than the person they want to be.

When you're in a relationship with someone—romantic, friendship, familial, or otherwise—you build your consent framework through communication and experience. It's a natural part of the relationship process. Sometimes it can be difficult to talk about things with people. That's natural too. And it is important to be able to do so. Here is an exercise that can help.

Skill Building: Tough Talk

Before you approach a difficult conversation, start with a personal inventory to define what it is you want to talk about.

What is the topic I need discuss?

_____

_____

With whom do I want to discuss it?

_____

_____

How do I feel about their potential reactions?

_____

_____

How will a positive reaction affect my life, short and long term?

How will a negative reaction affect my life, short and long term?

_____

_____

What am I trying to achieve?

_____

_____

What is my ideal outcome?

_____

_____

What assumptions am I making about the discussion?

_____

_____

What other issues or factors do I need to consider?

_____

_____

_____

_____

By preparing yourself mentally and emotionally, you can evaluate your feelings and assumptions ahead of time. Take the time you need to process possible outcomes, but focus on your ideal scenario.

Once you know what you want to say, to whom, and why, the next step is to figure out *how* and *when*. Here are some tips for creating the ideal exchange:

o **Create an Invitation**
   - Brainstorm a mutually agreeable time to talk. Launching into a tough topic when the other person is not prepared, tired, stressed, or distracted, will negatively impact your desired outcome.
   - Consider the nature of your relationship when deciding on a time and place. Is the conversation best had in private? In a public place? Do you need to have a timer on the conversation, or a back-up plan if the conversation doesn't go well?

- Make sure you have a plan for self-care or support for yourself after your conversation concludes.
- Create an environment of support and cooperation from the beginning. That starts with an invitation. It doesn't have to be formal, it can be as simple as one of the following questions:
    - "I need some support. Do you have some time?"
    - "I want to talk about _____. Can we have coffee tomorrow?"
    - "I need some help understanding _____. Can we talk about it?"
    - "I'd like to talk about something difficult. When is a good time for you?"

- **Augment Capacity**
    - Suspend assumptions about how they're likely to react.
    - Check in with the person and get consent before you start the conversation: "Is this still a good time?"
    - How are you feeling? Do you have any physical or emotional needs?
    - How is the other person feeling? Do they have any physical or emotional needs?
    - Eliminate distractions in your physical location, and make sure you can hear each other.

- **Create an Agreement**
    - Engage in active listening.
    - Let them know what you would like to see happen.
    - If needed, set ground rules for communication.
    - Confirm consent.

- **Share Information**
    - Be honest and open.
    - Avoid using euphemism, jargon, or sarcasm. Be clear.
    - Be willing to repeat or rephrase things if the other person has a hard time understanding.
    - Invite more discussion.

- **Make an Aftercare Plan**
    - Get support from someone else.
    - Take care of yourself physically: food, water, a nap, exercise, etc.
    - Take care of yourself emotionally: alone time, process time, distraction, etc.
    - Evaluate what happened.
    - Figure out what you want to do next.

Use the above suggestions to help draft a plan to make the discussion easier. Write the plan down if it will help. Remember to take your time and stay aware of the inventory you started with. Having a difficult conversation is tough, and it helps build strong relationships and better frameworks.

This chapter talked about public, professional, working, and intimate relationships. Throughout all of them, we build a framework to understand and interact with the people involved. No matter what the relationship is, consent is present and vital.

Without consent, and the frameworks we create, we are unable to form trust and connection. Through open and honest communication, and the willingness to have difficult conversations, we build our frameworks and the essential elements that allow those relationships to grow. With time—and practice—we use consent to build stronger, better understanding and connection.

And through those, we create the opportunity for respect, intimacy, love, and more.

Chapter 7: Consent and Sex

Why haven't we talked about sex yet?

You might—or might not—be surprised how many times we get asked that. People have been taught to think about consent only as it applies to sex or sexual behavior. As you have seen, consent is so much more than that. We wanted to give you a good grounding in concepts and ideas before we talked about the details of consent in a sexual context.

We believe the healthy way to talk about sex is directly and explicitly. This chapter will use specific sexual examples and terminology. We offer you the opportunity to consent by continuing to read this chapter, starting on the next page. If you would prefer not to, or would rather come back to it later, Chapter 8 starts on page 100.

Back to Basics

All the things we've already talked about apply when we're talking about sex and sexuality. Let's look at some important concepts about sex before getting into consent issues.

First, people have a wide range of feelings when it comes to sex. Some people feel good about their sex life and sexuality, while some feel ambivalence, and others feel shame. This can make it difficult to talk about sex.

As always, the place to start the conversation is with yourself. What are three words that describe how you feel about sex:

_____

_____

_____

How we feel about a topic determines how we think about it, which affects how we talk about it. When it comes to sex, if you feel a sense of shame, that will come out in both your communication and your attempts to give or receive consent. If you feel excited and happy, that will come out instead.

In the following spaces, list three words that describe how you want to feel about sex. Consider avoiding words that focus on shame and negativity. Instead think about words that focus on choice, autonomy, and positive framing.

_____

_____

_____

The next time you try to talk about sex, hold those words in your mind. Say them over and over to yourself as a way of reminding your brain how you want to feel about sex. Even if you don't say them aloud, this will help shape how you communicate.

Second, it is important to remember that sex is not just one thing. We are often taught that sex is one act: a male-identified person putting his penis into the vagina of a female-identified person (Penis-In-Vagina, or PIV sex). Sometimes sex is taught as PIV with the express intent of procreation. Certainly this is what most people learn when parents try (haltingly) to answer the question, "Where do babies come from?"

The reality is more complex. The term "sex" describes hundreds of behaviors engaged in by individuals, pairs, or groups of all different sexes, genders, ages, body types, and identities. It can be used to describe cuddling, masturbation, manual/digital sex, oral sex, vaginal intercourse, anal intercourse, frottage, BDSM play, use of sex toys, and the list goes on and on from there. Feel free to look up any of the above words you don't know, but maybe avoid the image search.

When we talk about sex, and getting consent around sex, we're not just talking about PIV sex. We're talking about all of the possible forms of sex. Try thinking of it this way: sex is any act where at least one of the people involved think of it as sex, experience sexual stimulation or pleasure, and/or use it for some type of sexual release.

Third, sex is different from sexuality. Sexuality is made up of all our desires, needs, pleasures, and concepts about sex. Sexuality is the identity around how you relate to sex, and it too involves many different behaviors, sexes, genders, ages, body types, and identities. Defining the difference between sex and sexuality would be a book in and of itself. For now, understand that we use the word "sex" to talk about a wide variety of sexual behaviors, and "sexuality" to talk about a wide variety of sexual identities.

Fourth, sex is intense. Some of you may be looking at this page and thinking, "Well, duh!" But this needs to be made explicit. When we think about sex, have desire for sex, experience feelings about sex, talk about sex, an engage in sex, we do so at an elevated state of physical, mental, and emotional arousal.

This increase in arousal has some dramatic effects on our brains and bodies. Physically, it changes blood flow, hormone and neurochemical production, and increases heart rate, respiration, and blood pressure. Mentally, it decreases concentration, perception, cognition, and inhibition. Emotionally, it increases intensity, emotional connectivity, and willingness to take risks.

Not everyone experiences this in the same way. For a variety of reasons, not everyone experiences sexual arousal. For those who do, however, the body is biologically geared towards a sexual response when presented with sexual stimuli.

The more sexually engaged you are, the less capacity you have for making decisions, regulating your emotions, and cognitively processing what is happening. Your body becomes directed towards an intense physical activity, and focused on the experience—ideally pleasurable—of that activity. As you can guess, and as we stated earlier, this diminishes the capacity for consent.

Which is why, regardless of the context, sexual activity is automatically in a higher risk category for Consent Incidents and Violations. There is always some increase in intensity, even just thinking about sex, that leads to a diminishment of capacity. It is part of being human.

Finally, intensity is not automatically a bad thing. Those heightened feelings can make sex more pleasurable and exciting. It doesn't make sex wrong or bad. In fact, we think sex can be quite good, and offers positive benefits like pleasure, connection, and positive expression of the self, when engaged in consensually. It is, however, complex and inherently more risky.

When you do engage in sexual activity, even when just talking about it, slow down. Real sex is not what we see in media or pornography. It takes time to do it well. It takes time to talk about it in real, authentic, and explicit ways, and it takes time to make sure both you and your partner(s) want to be there and are engaged in the activities and the communication.

Taking things a little slower, giving both you and your partner(s) time to process and experience what's happening, will help keep things consensual and reduce risk. It has also been shown to increase the opportunity for pleasure, so you have multiple reasons to take your time. It will help, we promise.

Sex and Capacity

Any sexual activity boosts physical, mental, and emotional arousal. This decreases capacity and increases risk. Remember though, increased risk is not inherently bad; it is something to pay attention to.

So, what does this look like? Imagine you want something simple, like a cookie you smell coming from the kitchen. The cookies are on top of the oven cooling, but you want to ask before decapitating the gingerbread man with your teeth. So you spend time thinking about how to ask for it, what your friend's responses are likely to be, and how to counter those responses. Because you want the cookie, you create a whole scenario in your mind that leads to you getting the cookie. You imagine having it and how it will taste.

Prepared to have what you now think of as "your" cookie, you go and ask your friend if you can have it. Before you even ask the question, simply because you want it, you have changed your perception from the cookie being something that is offered, to something you deserve. When you then ask for it, the other person may feel pressured or even coerced into giving you the cookie.

Now, if you can, imagine someone with whom you want to have sex. Imagine all the good things about it and what it would feel like. How does that change things? What happens to your level of emotional and physical arousal? How do you think that will change the way you react to someone when asking them for sex?

The simple act of wanting something creates a series of mental and emotional biases all geared towards getting us the thing we want:

- **Perception Bias:** We are more likely to see/hear things that match what we want, and less likely to see/hear the things that don't match.
- **Emotional Perception Bias:** We are more likely to see/hear emotions similar to what we're feeling, even when the other person isn't feeling that way. We are less likely to see/hear emotions that disagree or are opposed to what we're feeling.
- **Confirmation Bias:** We are more likely to see/hear things that agree with what we want, and less likely to see/hear the things that don't agree.
- **Control Bias (or the Illusion of Control):** We are more likely to believe we have greater control over a situation or external events than we do. This includes control over other people's desires and decisions.
- **Superiority Bias:** We tend to overestimate our own desirable qualities, and underestimate our undesirable qualities, relative to others.

Not everyone engages in these biases all the time, but people are more likely to engage in biased thinking in pursuit of something they want. This, in part, is what creates a reduction in capacity around consent. The very act of wanting something makes us more likely to mis-read or misunderstand the situation.

Biased thinking and the physiological effects of arousal come into play around sexual activities. The more intense the emotion or activity, the greater the impact on capacity. This in turn leads to a greater risk of Consent Incidents. And that's before we add in additional factors like substances, physical reductions, emotional reductions, and power dynamics.

This is true for both you and anyone else you're involved with, whether they are the person asking or the person being asked. Where sex and desire are involved, they are experiencing the same issue of capacity reduction you are. Understand that while they may not be impaired, their capacity is still diminished. Ask yourself if you are willing to accept the risks involved, and what you can do to help mitigate those risks.

Yes, it is complex, but there is hope. People negotiate sex successfully all the time. With good consent practices, it can be even better.

Sex and Informed Consent

People have a wide range of understanding and knowledge when it comes to sex. At younger ages, when we'r forming our concepts about how the world works, sex is rarely discussed. When sex is discussed, so little information is given that it tends to cause more confusion.

It's impossible to know what someone else knows unless you ask them and they're willing to talk about it. W will have guesses based on social scripts and preconceived ideas, but it is unlikely those guesses will be accurate.

Story: Sexual Misunderstandings

James and Susan have been married for 12 years. They have 2 kids, stressful jobs, and a lackluster sex life. James watches porn when Susan goes out of town, but is too ashamed to talk about it. Susan occasionally pays for an "intimate massage" just to feel the spark of arousal caused by someone else's touch, but is too ashamed to admit it, and is afraid it might be cheating.

After years of decreasing libidos and infrequent sex, the couple decides to "spice things up." They start with a little rope and a blindfold, which goes well. With more confidence, both turn to the internet for new, "hot" ideas.

One day Susan comes home from a shopping expedition and asks James if he would like to try anal sex. James, though he had watched it hundreds of times in porn, never thought she would be open to it. Aroused by the idea, and the images in his head, he quickly agrees and makes arrangements for the kids to stay with the grandparents.

That night in the bedroom, James can barely wait to get things started, tearing off his clothes and jumping into bed. As Susan goes into the bathroom to get ready, he thinks about how an anus might feel different from a vagina, and enjoys the thrill of potentially doing something "naughty." Already erect, he turns as he hears the door open.

Susan, blushing furiously, stands in the doorway wearing a strap-on and holding a bottle of lube.

The story, while amusing, shows how a different understanding of the term "anal sex" created a different expectation. Whether or not they went on to have a good evening (they did by the way), the encounter highlight the need for good information. Had Susan asked James if he wanted to try pegging, he might have had a better idea of what he was getting into. Had James asked what she meant, they might have had a more intimate discussion and been more prepared.

When thinking about having sex with someone, one of your first questions should be, "What do I know in th situation?" This includes what you know about yourself: your own needs, desires, experience, and knowledge. It also includes what you know about the other person: their wants, needs, experience, and knowledge. Lastly, it includes what you know about the activity itself: the environment, the highlights, the risks, and what you might need for it.

Because there is so little good sex education, we often don't know as much as we think. Even sex educators who spend decades studying sex and sexuality will admit they don't know all there is to know. The subject is just too broad. It's important to cultivate a sense of curiosity and "beginner's mind" about sex to help avoid assumptions and misunderstandings.

You need to have good information about what you are agreeing to before you can give clear and honest agreement. Having that information is what allows you to be honest both with yourself and the other person (or people) involved.

Sex and Agreement

When it comes to sex, this is where educators spend most of their time talking about consent. They talk about the importance of getting a clear yes or no before proceeding. However, as we talked about in Chapter 4, it is a lot more complicated.

The act of wanting something has a significant impact on our ability to accurately perceive the situation. The same is true of having a strong negative reaction or significant emotional trigger. This also makes it harder to be clear, and changes perception.

When giving or receiving boundaries around sex, it's good to be as clear as possible. Any no, or lack of an explicit and/or enthusiastic yes, means stop. There is no need to confirm it or ask more questions. The other person doesn't want sex, or that type of sex, or to continue the sex you were having. Consent is either withheld or withdrawn. Stop!

If you continue to engage in sex or sexual behavior after consent is withheld or withdrawn, you are committing an act of violation, assault, and rape.

Where there is confusion or misunderstanding, this is also the same as a no. Do not have sex. Remember, the more emotionally involved you are, the harder it is to see ambiguity or confusion, and it is easier to engage in confirmation bias. Ask open and clarifying questions to try to better understand:

- o I'm confused. Can you tell me what you want or don't want?
- o I want to make sure I understand. Can you tell me more?
- o Are you willing to say more?
- o My understanding of what we were talking about is (insert clear and explicit paraphrase of what was being discussed). Is that something you would like to do, or did you have something else in mind?
- o I want to (insert clear and explicit sexual act here). Is that something you want, too? Do you want something else?

In general, any question that gives the person the option to tell you more, but avoids indicating judgement about the answer, will be helpful. Both yes and no need to be equally good and valid responses.

When giving or receiving agreement around sex, it's good to take more time and confirm your understanding. Pay attention to your partner's body language for cues about how they are doing. Ask in multiple ways if your partner is sure if they want to continue:

- o "Do you want to continue?"
- o "Is this good?"
- o "I really want to (insert clear and explicit sexual act you already agreed to here). May I continue?"
- o Allow a nonverbal pause where you're paying attention to the body language and facial expressions of the other person. Wait for them to indicate a desire to continue.
- o "Yes?"

In general, any question that gives the person a moment to consider and then indicate that they want to continue—or stop—will be helpful.

People often talk about ruining the mood by "asking too many questions," as though wanting your partner to be comfortable and certain is a bad thing. If this is a worry, instead try focusing on making sure your partner is having a good and enjoyable time. You could try:

- o Taking several moments to watch your partner: their face, how they're moving, or how they're reacting.
- o Engaging in more non-erogenous/non-stimulating touch (with consent).
- o Engaging in sexual or "dirty" talk (with consent).
- o Asking them what they might like or find arousing.
- o Asking them to tell you their sexual fantasies.
- o Or just talk with them about whatever they want to talk about.

Sexual time doesn't always need to be about sex. Sometimes it's just about being human. Use that time to learn more about your partner, update your consent framework, and pay attention. This focus should lend itself to slowing down and getting additional input.

Ideally, agreement for sex should be clear, easy to understand, explicit, and enthusiastic. It should include some verbal statement similar to, "Hell, Yes!" "Absolutely!" or "Fuck me, now!" Additionally, the person's body language and behavior should match what they are saying verbally. This can include seductive posing, sexual positioning, and getting naked. All these things show explicit and enthusiastic agreement. (Be advised, however, that just nudity by itself, without an explicit agreement about sexual acts, should not be considered an invitation to engage sexually.)

It's important to note that many people use arousal characteristics, such as an erection, vaginal lubrication, engorgement of the vulva, nipple erection, a sexual flush, and other physical reactions as an indication of desire and/or consent for sex. However, these do not equal consent. They are physiological reactions to sexually relevant information, and cannot be used in place of an explicit and/or enthusiastic yes. "Sexually relevant information" means seeing, hearing, touching, tasting, or smelling something that is explicitly sexual—for example, watching someone masturbate. Men or male-bodied people often have stories of erections at inappropriate times when they don't want to have sex; women or female-bodied people are capable of this same experience, but can more easily hide and ignore it—our physical bodies do not always match what we actually want. Some of these signals may also be present as a reaction to fear.

In addition, there are people who, for a variety of reasons, have an absent or diminished physical sexual response. This lack of response does not automatically indicate a lack of desire or inability to consent. Always get verbal, signed, or written consent, ideally with congruent and enthusiastic behavior.

In another complication, people can have mixed feelings about what they're doing. They might think that being clear about wanting sex is somehow wrong. (Please know, it's not wrong. Wanting sex is perfectly normal. Not wanting sex is perfectly normal. Being true to yourself is what's important.)

With such confusion, agreement may not be as explicit or enthusiastic. A person might say, "Yes," but still look shy or hesitant. A person might use a Coded Yes, but show enthusiasm with their body. Sex is often complicated.

If you're the person saying yes, do your best to be clear. Be as enthusiastic as possible, and be willing to state your yes several times. If you find yourself having difficulty, you'll know that this is something to work on. If being enthusiastic is challenging, be sure to be explicit. Confront issues of shame and confusion by reflecting on what you truly want, talking with people who can support you, and practicing being open and honest wherever you have the chance.

If you're the person receiving a yes, do your best to pay attention and be open with your questions. Remember to take your time. If either of you is confused, you don't have consent. Step back and start over, even if it means you're not going to have sex in that moment. Taking the time to communicate builds trust and insures there will more opportunity for future sexy moments.

Ideally, boundaries in sex should also be clear, easy to understand, explicit, and enthusiastic. They should include verbal statements like: "No," "No way," "Not right now," or "Hell no!" Additionally, the person's body language should match what they are verbally saying. This can include closed body language (crossed arms, legs pulled together, lack of eye contact, etc.), defensive positioning (turning or backing away, arms up, clenched fists, etc.), and pushing away gestures. All these things show explicit and emphatic boundaries.

In the real world, boundaries around sex are not always clear. Just like when saying yes, people can have mixed feelings. This could include wanting to have sex, but not right now; feeling it's unsafe to say no; overwhelming shame; simple confusion; or any number of things that block desire. A person might try to say no, but it ends up unclear or confusing.

Watch for these signs, either before or during sex, that show a person doesn't want to continue:

- o A verbal no of any variety
- o Hesitation sounds or statements: "Uh... " "Ah... " "Um... " "So..."
- o Pushing away
- o Shaking of the head
- o Refusing to make eye-contact
- o Covering the genitals, chest, or mouth with hands or objects
- o A complete lack of movement
- o Significant muscle tension, especially around the eyes, jaw, or genitals
- o Wincing or making pain noises
- o Crying or screaming
- o Anything that gives an impression of discomfort, pain, or distress

Any of the above signs mean **<u>stop what you're doing immediately</u>**. It may not mean you need to stop having sex entirely—for instance, some people cry during sex for a number of reasons—but it does mean you need to stop what you're doing in the moment and check in. You need to find out if they still want to continue, and if you still have consent. If they can't give you explicit and/or enthusiastic consent, or if you no longer feel like you have enough consent to continue, *stop*!

There are two things that complicate sex even more. First, over time we build consent frameworks with our lovers the same way we do with other people. We learn through conversation and experimentation what they like and don't like. We learn what they are likely and unlikely to consent to.

In longer term relationships, getting consent for sex may look as simple as asking, "So, our usual Tuesday night?" This could be answered with a nod. To an outsider, this does not look informed, explicit, or enthusiastic. In a first time situation, it wouldn't be. But where two (or more) people have a long history together, they naturally use shorthand and experience to define the bounds of consent.

This doesn't mean consent isn't important in long-term relationships. It is just as important as every other interaction you have. If someone sets a boundary to something, even though they've agreed hundreds of times before, the boundary is still valid and needs to be respected. Consent is still given or withheld. It is still received and honored. The conversation around it is simply more subtle, based on personal history, and rooted in mutual trust.

People's needs, desires, and arousal mechanisms do change over time, as do their bodies, emotional reactions, and identities. Having an explicit conversation every 4-6 months helps to make sure consent is still present and active. It also gives you a great chance to practice open, honest, and explicit consent behavior. Practice rocks!

The second complication includes sexual practices like BDSM (Bondage, Discipline, Dominance, Submission, Sadism, Masochism) and sexual roleplaying. In these types of situations, consent is often established ahead of time, so that behaviors that would look like the withdrawal of consent to an outsider, continue to be consensual.

This could look like a lot of different things. The realms of BDSM and sexual roleplay are vast, and better covered in other books. The important thing to remember is that these activities are still consensual when explicit and/or enthusiastic consent is established before the sexual act is engaged in.

These situations often use a "safeword" or "safesign" so participants can indicate a withdrawal of consent. This is often a word, phrase, or gesture that is out of context of the scene being played, and therefore a clear indication to stop and/or check in. Some common ones include: Safeword, Red, Yellow, some non sequitur word like "peppermint," or use of a person's real or full name. The specific word is less important than making sure everyone involved understands that it means stop, and that consent is being withdrawn.

Because BDSM and sexual roleplaying often take place at a high level of physical, emotional, and sexual intensity, the people who practice this type of sex tend to be more aware of and interested in consent. Practitioners have created a variety of consent practices to help make sure the people playing are safe and respected throughout. Even with that heightened awareness, mistakes are still made and people's consent is violated. It is important to maintain an explicit and well-polished consent practice when engaging in these types of activities.

Even though getting agreement often happens before moving into action, it's important to think of it as an ongoing process. When having sex with someone, consent is renewed constantly and continuously. Which also means it can be withdrawn at any time and for any reason. Understanding this, and respecting it when it happens, is part of respecting our sexual partners and their autonomy.

Sex and Autonomy

As we discussed in Chapter Five, autonomy is the right to make decisions about what is done to and with your body, mind, and spirit. It is the right to make decisions for yourself. Where this applies to sex is simple in concept, and difficult in practice.

When autonomy is respected, you have the freedom to make decisions for yourself, based on your own needs and desires. It also means you have the time and space to figure out what those are. It means you get to request the sex you want, and say no to the sex you don't want.

When autonomy is respected, you have freedom from people trying to change your decisions. You needn't worry about people trying to force you to do what they want or coerce you into changing your mind. You get to make an honest decision, and know people will accept it.

When autonomy is respected, your statements will be taken at face value. If you say yes to something, people will honor that and believe you have the right to choose it for yourself. If you say no, people will respect it the first time, believe that you have the right to make that decision, and won't question it.

All of these statements about autonomy also apply to sex, sexuality, and sexual behavior. All possible sexual choices, from abstinence to orgy, will be equally okay as long as they are consensual. All possible sexualities, sexual expressions, and sexual identities will be equally ok as long as they are consensual. You will be free from having these questioned, ridiculed, or shamed simply because they involve sex.

Again, this sounds simple in concept, yet human beings are rarely simple.

We all experience times when our autonomy is not upheld. Most of us have had that experience around sex and sexuality as well. We have been questioned, or shamed, or coerced into behavior we didn't want. Sometimes it is done to us, and sometimes we do it to ourselves.

Understanding sexual autonomy helps in three ways.

First, it helps us to understand our right to make honest and autonomous decisions about our own sexual behavior. This is something many people try to undermine or diminish. They do it for economic, political, religious, or personal gain. But they do not get to tell you who to be or what to consensually do. That is for you to decide.

Second, understanding sexual autonomy helps us know when someone is hurting us. Knowing what autonomy should be helps to point out when it's not happening. Practicing our own autonomy gives us a sense of how things should feel. That way when someone isn't respecting ours, we have a better chance of realizing it. Then, once realized, we can either state better boundaries, leave the situation, or do our best to reduce the harm we absorb.

Third, it helps us treat people better. Knowing how to recognize the autonomy of others, even when there is something we want, gives us the opportunity to respect and honor other people. Practicing the skill of recognizing and honoring autonomy helps us avoid causing harm. In sex, it also encourages us to find out what our partner(s) want or don't want.

When we get horny or experience shame, we have a hard time holding on to complex concepts. Preserving autonomy, either for ourselves or someone else, is just more difficult when we get emotionally activated.

This is why it's important to practice, both in and out of sexual situations. The more practice you have, the easier it will be. The more you talk about autonomy, or sex, the more you will understand your own part in it. You will have an opportunity to not only feel better about yourself, but to have a better understanding of your lovers, and potential lovers, as well.

How to Know When You have Consent During Sex

Let's put all of this together. Here are a couple vignettes of what sexual consent looks like.

Story: Sexual Consent – Hooking Up

After a long week, Mark is out looking to let off steam and find someone to hook up with. At a bar, he is chatting while switching back and forth between Tinder and Grindr on his phone. A match comes up—someone he thinks is cute—and he steps outside.

Ten minutes later he's heading to a different bar. He meets up with Stan and the two of them talk. There's chemistry and obvious interest. Both men are open, flirting, and reaching out with small touches. They have a couple of drinks.

Mark asks Stan back to his place. Stan agrees.

In the car on the way back, Mark confirms he is only looking for something that night, nothing long term. Stan nods and cups Mark's balls, pausing just a second and waiting until Mark leans in.

The two men continue to flirt, getting more and more bold as they reach the end of the ride. Once there, Stan takes a picture of the apartment and texts it to a friend with the address, making a "just in case" joke. Before they go up, he asks Mark if he has condoms. Mark smiles and says, "Oh yeah. Plenty."

In the elevator Mark asks, "Anything I need to worry about?"

"A mind-blowing orgasm?" Stan answers, and they both laugh. "Seriously though, I have HSV-1, but no outbreaks. Other than that, my last tests were negative a month ago, and no worries since. You?"

Mark smiles, "I'm good too. Last test was in June, and negative across the board. So, what do you want?"

Stan follows him to his apartment. "You, and some good sex."

"I think we can manage that."

"You?"

"Same. No hitting or slapping, though. I had a guy over last spring who thought that was foreplay."

Stan takes off his shirt and begins unbuttoning Mark's pants. "I think I can do better. Ready?"

Mark starts working on Stan's belt. "Hell yes!"

Story: Sexual Consent – Love & Baked Goods

Marta and Rick have been dating for three months. They met online and connected over a love of French baking. The relationship grew slowly, from dates at bakeries all over town, to baking late into the night in Marta's kitchen.

The two enjoyed each other's company, but both were shy. Rick had gotten out of a bad marriage a couple years before, and Marta hadn't had a serious boyfriend in a while. They both wanted it to work.

Last week, Rick broached the subject of being sexual, and Marta quickly agreed. The two talked about their pasts and revealed some sexual history. Rick had never had an STI test, and agreed to get one. Marta showed the results from her last screening.

The two chatted over the week, flirting and being more sexual with one another. Marta shared she likes oral sex, both giving and receiving, and waited nervously until Rick replied with a thumbs up and an eggplant emoji. Rick forwarded the results from his tests, and told her how much he was looking forward to being with her. They agreed on some boundaries, and to meet at Marta's place on Saturday.

Marta cleaned the house and prepared for the evening. When Rick arrived, there were candles lit, soft music playing, and a stack of eclairs on the table. The two fumbled, flirted, and laughed for an hour. There was even a cliche whipped cream moment.

Ready, Marta led Rick to the bedroom where there were more candles. Condoms were already laid out on the bedside table. "I really want you."

Breath catching in his throat, he whispered back, "I really want you too."

They slowly undressed each other, leaning in for kisses and hesitant touches. Eventually they made it to the bed, kissing more and talking less. As Marta reached to caress Rick's penis, he froze and said, "It's been a while for me."

Marta smiled, and said, "I guessed. You told me about your ex. How about we start with something we both want?" She slid down him, and, mouth hovering over the tip of his penis, licked her lips.

Rick nodded enthusiastically. "Are you sure?"

Marta wrapped her lips around him and mumbled, "Um huh."

Some time—and an orgasm—later, Rick was more relaxed and reached for the condoms. He felt Marta freeze against him, and he pulled back. "Are you okay?"

She tried to hide her tears, but couldn't. "I'm sorry. I thought I was ready for more."

"Shhhhh." He put a hand on her shoulder and waited for her to relax. "It's okay, there's no rush."

"You don't hate me?"

"No, I don't hate you. You were amazing when I felt scared. I just want to do the same for you."

"You sure?"

"Yeah, I'm sure. We don't have to do anything you don't want."

Marta's body relaxed against him and they held each other. After a time she started rubbing up against him, feeling more aroused. He noticed and responded by kissing her neck.

Marta, feeling uncertain, but interested, said, "I'm not up for, you know, intercourse tonight. I just need more time."

"It's okay."

She leaned up on one elbow, "But if you're interested, you could go down on me." Feeling him tense, she added, "Or I can go down on you again."

He let out a deep breath. "No, I'd like to.... at least try. I, uh, don't have a lot of experience."

"Only if you're sure. I can go slow too."

He thought for a moment. "Yeah, I'd like to try."

"Okay. Why don't you start by..."

What did you think of those two stories? What met your expectations, and what was different?

_____

_____

Where did consent show up in the story between Mark and Stan?

_____

_____

Where did consent show up in the story between Rick and Marta?

_____

_____

What could have been done better?

_____

_____

_____

What would you have done?

_____

_____

_____

Now think of a story from your own life. Think of a time when you engaged in getting and giving sexual consent.

Where did consent show up in that story?

_____

_____

_____

What could have been done better?

_____

_____

_____

Knowing what you know now, what would you have done differently?

_____

_____

_____

Few situations are perfect. Sex is messy in all sorts of ways. The goal is to practice consent as best you can, and deal with situations as they arise. Doing that and focusing on being present with your partner(s) will help you be more consensual *and* better at sex. Win-Win.

How to have Better Consent during Sex

How are you feeling after all that discussion of sex and sexual consent? Scared? Worried? Angry? Horny?

All of these are normal and understandable reactions. This is a complicated subject and it can be hard to process—much like sex itself. Here is a list, in all its wonderful complexity, of ways to help sex be more consensual:

1. **Slow down**. As we said before, it's important to take your time when thinking, talking about, and engaging in sex. Taking more time to process and communicate about what you're doing will help increase capacity.
2. **Negotiate and make agreements ahead of time.** Negotiate what you want to do sexually before your level of arousal overwhelms you or your partner. Even hours or days before can work well.
3. **Don't renegotiate for more in the middle of sex.** Stick to what you both consented to. Don't ask to do more, and stop if your partner tries. It is okay to renegotiate for less.

4. **Be willing to stop or walk away.** If anything feels off, isn't working for you, or doesn't feel good, stop what you're doing. Pause. Then talk about it. If pausing and talking isn't helping, stop altogether. Where necessary, walk away.

5. **Know and talk about the sex you want, and the sex you don't want.** Share with your partner what feels good to you, what your fantasies are, and what has worked for you in the past. Share what doesn't feel good, what your sexual boundaries are, and what has gone poorly in the past.

6. **Talk about expectations.** What are you expecting from the other person? What are they expecting from you?

7. **Use clear and specific language.** Make sure your language is accurate and understandable. Avoid euphemisms and vagaries. If you want to have intercourse, say that. If you want to have cunnilingus (oral sex on a vulva), say that. Avoid hints or suggestions. It doesn't need to be scientific language—you can use sexy, slutty, or whatever type of language you want—but it needs to be clear.

8. **Talk about sexual risk factors.** Make sure you talk about potential risk factors:

    a. Current STI (Sexually Transmitted Infection) status. This may require getting tested before having sex.

    b. Any STI risk factors (such as other partners) or behaviors (like sharing needles for drug use).

    c. Any physical or emotional injuries or risks that could be impacted by the sex you are choosing to have.

    d. Any relationship issues or expectations that could be impacted by the sex you are considering.

    e. Use of condoms or other barrier protection and their availability.

    f. Use of contraception (prevention of an unwanted pregnancy) and what will happen if a pregnancy should occur.

9. **Understand other potential risk factors.** Make sure to consider other things that might impact your decision:

    a. *Timing:* Make sure you have enough time to make the decisions you need, and to enjoy yourself.

    b. *Location:* Consider if the space where you're going to have sex is safe and comfortable enough. Consider if there preparations you should make first.

    c. *Power Differentials:* Take the time to reflect on any differences in the level of power or agency between the people involved. Consider how to address the difference, if there is one.

    d. *Substance use:* If alcohol, drugs, or other substances are being used during sex, learn how they impact the people involved. Consider how to reduce harm or risk.

    e. *Type of Sex:* Talk about the type of sex or specific behaviors you're going to be having. Explore potential risks and how to reduce potential harm.

    f. *Type of Relationship:* Review any relationship concerns or issues involved in the sex you are having.

10. **Negotiate clearly and openly.** Make sure everyone involved knows what is being agreed to, and is able to follow the agreement. Where there is complexity or increased risk, write the agreement down so all parties understand what is being agreed to and can make changes where needed.

11. **State your agreement or boundary clearly and explicitly.** Take the time you need to make a decision, and then state that decision in a way other people can understand. Reinforce where necessary.

12. **Take any confusion or lack of answer as a no.** Only an explicit and/or enthusiastic yes means you have consent. Anything else means consent does not exist. Where appropriate, ask open-ended questions to resolve confusion. Avoid asking more than twice.

13. **Respect any no, or boundary stated.** Avoid questioning why the person made the boundary. Avoid pushing against the boundary. Accept it whenever it is given, either before or during sex.

14. **Stop when you don't have consent.** If you don't have consent, or if someone has withdrawn consent, stop whatever you're engaged in, or don't start in the first place.

15. **Respect autonomy.** Everyone has the right to decide what to do with their body. And they have the right to make the decision without coercion or undue influence. Practice respecting both your own autonomy, and that of others.

16. **Practice consent whenever you have the chance.** Practicing consent in your daily life will make it easier to do when you're having strong feelings or arousal. The more you do it, the easier it will be.

17. **Slow down.** Did we say that already? Ah well, it bears repeating. Take your time, figure out what's right for you, and find out what's right for your partner(s). Consent and communication both require more time, but the time is well worth it.

Consent is important and complex in all areas of life. While it's not more important in sex and sexual situations, it is more complex. The intensity, lack of education, and risk of harm all come together to make the practice of consent vital. When you're having sex, or even talking about having sex, make sure your consent practice is strong. To do otherwise risks harm and the consequences that go along with it.

Chapter 8: What to Do When Consent Goes Wrong

We can do everything right and consent can still go wrong. It's not a question of if you will make a mistake, i is a question of when. It's not a question of if consent will be violated, it is a question of when.

Unfortunately, even with all of the information we've provided, consent can go wrong. Many conditions create positive or negative consent interactions in our lives: relationship dynamics, environment, internal motivators, capacity issues, etc. The impact of your actions can affect others in ways you aren't expecting. Even when our *intent* is pure and positive, the *impact* can still be negative.

In this chapter, we will identify different motivations and assess the level of risk that can lead to Consent Incidents. By assessing your level of risk, you can make better choices about how (and/or if) you want to engage with another person. We'll also have tips on what to do if you violate someone's consent, and how to handle it when your consent is violated.

Everyone has had their consent violated at some point. (Remember to think of consent as an everyday occurrence.) Many of those violations were small and barely noticed, while others left scars or trauma. Also, we have all violated someone else's consent at some point. Many of those instances were small and barely noticed. Some left scars or shame.

This may be a difficult and emotional chapter. Take your time and pause when you need to. Remember, this book is about understanding consent, in all of its complexity, and working to do it better. Looking at times when things don't work out, and what to do about it, is just as important as building the skills to avoid making mistakes.

Consent Incident vs Consent Violation

First, we need to define some terms to help talk about the complexity around when consent goes wrong. Because it is such an emotional topic, we find that more technical language can help the discussion.

A **Consent Incident** is an event, involving consent, where something has gone wrong. In a Consent Incident, there is no assumption of intention, guilt, or fault. Just as there is no assumption of victim or perpetrator, there is no assumption of harm or trauma. This is an event that needs consideration, review, and outside support. When a Consent Incident occurs we want to understand what happened, and figure out what to do next.

A **Consent Violation** is an event where a person believes their consent was *broken*, a set boundary was *crossed*, or lasting *harm* was caused during a Consent Incident. Only the person who experiences the event gets to decide if their consent was violated. There is no external assumption of intent, while still recognizing that harm has been caused. This means that everyone does their best to avoid assigning "blame" or "fault," and assumes that the person who did the actions that negatively affected someone else **did not mean to cause harm** with their actions. All parties involved deserve emotional support, social support, education, and sometimes intervention by an organization or team. When a Consent Violation occurs, the goal is to find ways of reducing the impact to the affected party, and preventing the harm from happening again.

Both Consent Incidents and Consent Violations exist on a spectrum. On one end we have micro-transgressions: small consent issues with little impact in the moment; these might include stepping on someone's foot, neglecting to ask if it's ok to interrupt, or commenting on someone's appearance without asking first. In the middle are incidents such as touching, hugging, taking a picture, or sharing a story without another's permission. On the other end are major transgressions, consent issues that can have significant and lasting impact; examples of these are stealing, physical assault/battery, sexual assault, and rape.

Remember, only the person impacted gets to define how significant something is for them. What might be significant for one person, might be minor for another. **We don't get to define that for them. They get to define it for themselves.**

Talking about consent on this type of spectrum gives more room for dialogue without fear and defensiveness. **When all Consent Violations are lumped into the severe side of the spectrum, it makes it difficult to discuss the less-impactful ones openly.** It helps to remember that we have all violated consent at some point, and we want to improve—that's why you're reading this book!

Most people do not intentionally violate consent. Most Consent Incidents are created through misunderstanding, lack of attention, or faulty assumptions. Many can be resolved by asking questions, gathering information, and setting boundaries. These incidents may still cause harm, but it helps to approach them with understanding and lack of assumption about intent.

The ability to identify the difference between an intentional versus an unintentional transgression, as well as the motivations of others, is hard—sometimes impossible. We rarely know what another person is thinking or feeling. We do know how we feel, and often, the more hurt or upset we are, the more likely we are to believe the harm done was done intentionally.

Additionally, identifying the difference between an intentional versus an unintentional transgression may not be necessary. Sometimes if something hurts or harms you, that's what needs to be addressed and dealt with. In any incident, it is good to consider intent or lack thereof—**but it is more important to get support and deal with what happened.**

When something goes wrong and your consent has been violated, slow down as much as possible. Take time to breathe and assess the situation. Get the support you need, and recognize that it may take time to deal with it. When you are able, work to process the incident and figure out what you need (from yourself or others) in order to take care of yourself.

As you gather more information, your perceptions may alter. Sometimes there are other factors which weren't apparent in the moment. The perceived motivations of others, past experiences, and your own capacity all have a huge impact on how you process a Consent Incident.

When consent has been broken, it takes time to identify it. Any issue involving consent is a Consent Incident, but only the person harmed can say if it's a Consent Violation. If you're the one harmed, make that determination after learning as much about the event as possible and processing your pain. If you are upset, angry, or hurting, it will be hard to use "beginner's mind" and maintain a sense of curiosity. Without this, taking steps to protect yourself or others in the future may not be possible, and you may find yourself repeating behaviors that violate your own boundaries.

Being able to identify if it was an Incident will help you review and work on better boundaries for the future. Being able to identify it as a Violation will help you to process and get support. Take time to find your path forward. Remember, if you were the one hurt, it is not your fault; the other person's bad behavior was solely their decision.

Whether you determine it was a Violation or not, take a moment to give your future self the gift of wisdom and experience. Learn what you can from what happened, and make changes that will help keep you and/or others safer. Find the support you need and look for what to do next.

Intent vs Impact

Intent is the sum of our thoughts, feelings, desires, and beliefs that go into a decision to engage in a behavior. It can be either conscious or unconscious. Intent happens prior to an action, and may take minutes or fractions of a second to form. Once formed, intent is influenced by our physical, mental, and emotional capacities before it becomes a behavior. Intent is not the behavior that results: it is the driving force that causes a behavior.

Impact is the effect a behavior has. When a behavior is initiated by someone else, we perceive it, and then we have a response. Those thoughts and feelings are the **impact**. The response is influenced by our perception of the behavior, our current physical, mental, and emotional capacity, and our systems of belief and/or understanding. Impact is *not* the behavior it resulted from; impact is how the behavior lands within you. To put it another way, impact is not the actions done nor the words spoken by the other person; it is your *reaction* that arises in response to someone else's actions or words.

Intent does not always equal impact. One person can tell a joke they believe will be funny, but the person listening hates it. They may even find the joke offensive. This is one example of a time when the intent does not match the impact.

It's important to remember that both intent and impact can be true and valid, **even when they don't match**. Just because someone is hurt by something, doesn't mean the other person meant to hurt them. The harm is still valid. The lack of intent to cause harm is also valid. Holding this understanding can be difficult, but can lead to greater understanding and perspective.

It is not uncommon, in densely populated metropolitan areas, to experience someone on the street yelling. This can be caused by diminished capacity, due to stress, mental health, and/or substances. The yeller is not engaging in the agreements we hold as a society for acceptable public behavior. Depending on the emotion behind their vocal inflections, the words yelled, and your personal experiences, their actions can elicit different responses.

You may laugh, be frightened, get angry, or feel the need to get help. The person is most likely not yelling directly at you. They likely do not have the capacity at the moment to be aware of their actions. But their *intent* does not diminish the *impact* their actions have.

The emotional impact will influence how you will react. How you react and interact with the yeller depends on your own personal capacity. Is the yeller angry, or being funny? Are you the type to yell back? Do you have the time and skill set to approach the person? Would you need to leave the area and calm yourself?

How do you imagine you would react in this situation?

_____

_____

What factors (such as age, race, gender) would change your reaction?

_____

_____

Would you feel your consent has been personally violated?

_____

_____

What past experiences are in play to cause your reaction?

_____

_____

How would you take care of yourself after this interaction?

_____

_____

When we imagine the different scenarios, mitigating factors, and how to manage self-care after the experience, we can develop compassion for others who are struggling, and not *intentionally* trying to violate our consent. Knowing the things that impact you, and how to keep yourself emotionally safe in a situation like this is, not only good self-care, but involves taking excellent personal responsibility. We cannot control others, but we can control how we process and respond.

Understanding that intent is not the same as impact, and impact is not the same as intent, allows us to take a step back. It allows us to separate how we feel about the situation from our assumptions of what the other person meant to do. Ideally, it allows us to start approaching others with more curiosity regarding their experience and process.

Environmental Influences

Transgressions are not always so one-sided as a stranger yelling on the street. Any interaction with another person can include some form of behavior which leaves us feeling uncomfortable and might lead to a Consent Incident. They can be caused by some outside force within the environment.

For example, the person sitting next to you on the bus bumps into your arm every time the bus makes a turn. Your seatmate is not intentionally trying to touch you. The Consent Incident of being touched without your permission is unintentional and being caused by the movement of the bus, which is out of the control of your seatmate.

In this scenario, with the information available, you might consider this a Consent Incident, but not a Consent Violation. Your seatmate touched you without permission, yet there is an understandable explanation that does not involve their intent to violate your personal space.

The way you are impacted by this interaction depends on your capacity. If you are in a good mood and feeling physically fine, the *impact* won't have a lasting effect on you. If, however, you recently had an injury, and every time your seatmate bumps into your arm it sends shooting pain through your body, their *intent* is not to hurt you but the *impact* can make you feel violated.

This is where, by slowing down and engaging the understanding we have built, we can enter into a dialogue about what is happening.

Skill Building: Altering an Agreement in Public

Sticking with this particular scenario, there are many decisions you can make based on the information you have. You can decide your seatmate is intentionally causing you pain, feel violated, and get upset. You can decide that, although your seatmate is not intentionally causing you harm, you don't want the non-consensual interaction to continue, and physically remove yourself. Or, if you have built the skills to engage with a stranger, you can try negotiation.

Here's a possible example. Start by gauging **capacity** for communication. Try smiling and commenting on the bumpy ride.

1. If they have the capacity to hear you, understand what you are saying, and engage, you can continue the negotiation.

2. Give your seatmate more **information**: tell them what is happening, and how the physical interaction is causing you pain. Get them invested in a solution by letting them know you don't think they are intentionally trying to bump into you.

3. Negotiate a new **agreement** by making a request, such as asking to trade seats so your injured arm is not contacting their arm.

How do you envision this consent negotiation resolving? Is it a positive outcome?

_____

Can you imagine any factors which may cause the outcome to be negative?

_____

_____

Would you be comfortable trying this strategy?

_____

_____

Why or why not?

_____

Are there factors that would change your comfort level with this type of negotiation?

_____

_____

What area would you need to work on in your life to make this a skill you could use in different situations?

Being aware and taking into account how the environment is affecting your interactions is an important ski
Understanding how this can impact our perception of intent—before jumping to conclusions—can save a lot of
needless pain and suffering.

The Impact of Sharing Information

We all have personal information that, when shared, helps others honor our consent. It could be boundaries
things that are important to you, or information about your past. Information can be difficult to share for a
variety of reasons: how comfortable you are, the social or emotional impact, and your relationship to the person
you are sharing the information with, to name just a few.

Every day we make decisions on what to share. If you evaluate the information you want to share and the
circumstances around sharing it, you can better understand the potential difficulties, and your own possible
reactions to sharing your story.

Do you find it easy to share information about yourself?

_____

Why or why not?

_____

_____

What kinds of information would you only share with people you trust?

_____

_____

Who are those people in your life?

_____

_____

Is your potential risk for creating a Consent Incident increased or decreased by *not* sharing that
information?

_____

_____

What things could you share more of to help reduce your risk of Consent Incidents?

_____

_____

_____

Considering your personal reactions both raises your awareness about what is important to you, and defines your personal consent framework better. It can help you figure out what you're okay with sharing. It might also bring up memories of past rejection, harm, or other incidents. It you have never put together such an inventory, start with simple things. For example, you could start by thinking about what kind of hot beverage you enjoy. Is there something special about your drink that, if made incorrectly, could have serious impact on you? Are you willing to share this information with a select few, or everyone?

Fill out the example below, and then rate your comfort level with how easy it is for you to share that information with others on a scale from 1 (no trouble) to 10 (great distress).

What Beverage:

_____

How is it made:

_____

Why do you like it that way:

_____

Who needs to know the information:

_____

_____

Personal Comfort Rating (1-10)

_____

What feelings came up as you did this?

_____

_____

_____

Sharing what beverage you like and how you take it, generally speaking, isn't a sensitive topic. When you use the same process to make a list of more personal topics, such as relationship orientation or sexual preferences, may bring up more feelings. Consider trying the same exercise with something more personal. Some examples might be, "How clean do I like to keep my kitchen?" or, "What is my general state of mind when I wake up in the morning?"

Topic:

_____

What is important about it:

_____

_____

Why it's important:

_____

_____

Who needs to know the information:

_____

_____

Personal Comfort Rating (1-10)

_____

If the information is sensitive, shameful, or causes fear, get some help working through those feelings. Be gentle with yourself and with others. Any personal information can be hard to share depending on the dynamic and your past experiences.

It is up to you how, why, and with whom you share your personal details. Regardless, if you decide to share personal data or not, weigh the risks. Think about how you will take responsibility if a Consent Incident occurs because of withheld information.

When someone else has withheld information from you, think about some of the reasons they might do that. Consider how much trust you have between the two of you, and if that might be a factor. Where you can, ask them to take responsibility for the information they didn't share.

The Impact of Miscommunication

Miscommunication is a state where one person has expressed something, and another person has interpreted something different. One person intended to pass along a specific piece of information and the other received something else. Communication has been interrupted, information confused, and consent put at risk.

This happens for a wide variety of reasons, some of which were mentioned before, like language barriers. You might also consider awareness issues or technical glitches that may contribute to miscommunication. The information may get altered by passing through several sources. (Ever play a game of "telephone?") There may even be something as simple as two people having different meanings for the same word or phrase.

Whatever the reason, information can be miscommunicated. The person receiving the information either doesn't understand what was meant, or worse, incorrectly believes they *do* understand. That person then moves forward based on incorrect information.

When people are being open and honest with each other, this type of error is unintentional. The person giving the information intends to communicate it clearly. The person receiving the information intends to hear or see it. But something happens, and an error occurs.

Many of you have experienced what happens next. There is confusion. There is uncertainty. There may be frustration or anger. There may be accusation or argument. Where it involves consent, there may be hurt, an Incident, and/or a Violation.

Miscommunication happens. It is normal, and there are ways to deal with it.

- o Slow down and take your time.
- o Don't assume you have the correct information.
- o Check your understanding about what you think you know.
- o Get to know people and their communication styles before discussing difficult or risky things.
- o Practice active listening and paraphrasing skills.

When it comes to consent, do all of these. The more significant the consent or the greater the risk you're taking, the more important it is to slow down and practice good communication. And, when a miscommunication inevitably happens, understand that it is a mistake to be processed and managed.

Consent Mistakes

Error, inaccuracy, slip, blunder, oversight, gaffe, faux pas... Whatever you call them mistakes happen. We all make them. Sometimes they are avoidable, and other times not. Sometimes we have the best of intentions and still mess up.

When it comes to consent, mistakes are normal, much like they are in every other part of our lives. We make them, and they affect other people. They make them, and those mistakes affect us. As noted, the impact of those mistakes varies depending on the severity, the circumstances involved, and the state of the person impacted.

For those of you who have ever driven a car, or been a passenger in one, imagine driving down a road in the winter. Everything is going fine until you encounter a patch of ice. You try to stop, but end up hitting the car in front of you. A mistake. There is no intent to have an accident. It is a mistake made up of a series of decisions, circumstances, and potentially unforeseen events.

The impact varies widely based on how fast both cars were going, the physical health of the people involved, the state of the road, etc. There might be no damage. Someone, or multiple someones, might end up in the hospital. Perhaps the police are called.

Consent can be like that car accident. No one involved meant for a violation to happen, but it did. Someone got hurt.

Just like the car on an icy road, the person who caused harm is still responsible, even though it was a mistake. This can be hard to process and manage. The person harmed may see the harm as intentional. The person who caused the harmed may say it's not their fault. The important thing is for everyone to slow down, process, gather information, and own their individual responsibility for what happened. Then you can figure out what to do next.

Story: Mistakes Handled Poorly

Ji and Samantha are out on their third date. Tonight they have decided to try ice skating. Ji has been dozens of times, while Sam is brand new to the ice.

The two chat and flirt while getting their skates. Ji tells Sam about learning to skate as a kid, giving pointers for what to do when she gets on the ice. Sam gets her skates on and gives Ji a kiss on the cheek.

As Sam steps out on the ice, Ji gives her a playful swat on the ass. Sam squeaks, flails wildly, and lands on her face. Ji immediately rushes over to help.

Sam sits up, blood running out of her nose. "What the hell?"

Ji, taken aback, slips and falls too.

"First-off: what were you thinking, it's my first time. And secondly: who said you could touch my ass, much less spank me?"

Ji blushes, and reacts without thinking, saying, "It was a love pat. I barely touched you, and I didn't think you would fall. It's not my fault you lost your balance."

Furious, hurting both physically and emotionally, Sam stalks off the ice. She throws her skates to the attendant and leaves without another word.

Story: Mistakes Handled Well

Andy and Mason met a week ago at a party, and have gotten together for a date. Mason likes getting tied up, and has a social media profile full of sexy pictures. Andy is fairly new to bondage, but has taken a few classes. The two get along and there is chemistry between them.

They meet at Mason's house, negotiate a "just rope" scene, and check in about physical injuries and concerns. The basics out of the way, Mason undresses while Andy gets the rope ready.

Andy spends half an hour putting Mason into an elaborate chest harness. It is very attractive, and as Andy is checking the knots, he leans in and kisses Mason on the mouth.

Mason screams in surprise, and starts struggling against the rope. "Get me out! Let me go!"

Andy freaks out and freezes. This has never happened before. It takes a good twenty seconds, which feels like forever, to shake out of the paralysis. At which point, Andy grabs the safety scissors, helps Mason to the floor, and begins cutting the rope free.

Crying, Mason asks, "Why did you kiss me? Why?"

At a loss for words, Andy finishes removing the rope, and sits back. "I… I don't know. I just felt it."

"I didn't say you could kiss me. We didn't negotiate for that."

"I know. I'm sorry." Andy gets up, grabs a blanket and a bottle of water. Catching Mason's eye, Andy makes a pantomime of draping the blanket over Mason's shoulders, and Mason nods tearfully. He then adds, "And I'm sorry it took me so long to get you out. I just froze."

Mason takes the water and some long breaths. The tears stop, but their skin is still pale. "I don't mix sex and rope. Kissing is like sex."

"I didn't know." Andy takes a few deep breaths as well. "And I'm so sorry. You're right, I shouldn't have kissed you. My fault."

Mason visibly relaxes and looks around at the pile of now ruined rope. "Sorry about your rope. I just… it's a really strong reaction. I was…"

Andy holds up a hand. "You don't need to tell me right now. Let's get you back in your clothes, and then, when you're ready, tell me what else I can do to help."

Two stories. Both unintentional mistakes. Two different outcomes.

What was the Consent Incident in Ji and Sam's story?

_____

_____

Why do you think Sam reacted so negatively?

_____

_____

What was the Consent Incident in Andy and Mason's story?

_____

_____

What did Andy do that helped the situation?

_____

_____

What did Mason do that helped the situation?

Mistakes happen. How we handle those mistakes makes a big difference. If you're the one the mistake happens to, try the following:

- o Stop whatever you're doing and prioritize safety.
- o Focus on things you need for self-care.
- o You are probably going to have an emotional reaction. *That's okay.* Do what you can to regulate your reaction.
- o If needed, or possible, leave the situation/space where the mistake happened. Get some distance, both physically and emotionally.
- o Get support from someone else if you're not comfortable with getting support from the person who made the mistake.
- o Work on processing your own thoughts and feelings. Avoid assuming the other person made the mistake intentionally.

Afterwards, once you've had some time to process your feelings around it, see what you can do to manage what happened. Wait until your initial reaction has run its course before trying to communicate with the other person about it—even if that takes hours, days, or longer. Once you're ready, try some of the following:

- o Figure out if you need new or different boundaries.
- o Figure out what you need from the other person to resolve the mistake and/or reconnect.
- o Communicate what your new boundaries are, what your needs are, and what you expect from the other person. Be as clear as possible.
- o Listen to what they are willing to do, and evaluate if it matches your boundaries, needs, and expectations. If it does, great. If it doesn't, restate your position.
- o If things aren't working, and you still want to save the relationship, seek help from organizations, mediators, therapists, etc.
- o If, after more time and process, you still can't negotiate a resolution, accept that the relationship is not possible and move on.

If you're the one who made the mistake, try the following:

- o Stop what you're doing and prioritize safety. Do whatever you need to do to make sure both you and the other person are physically safe.
- o Give the other person space. Avoid physical contact unless it is explicitly requested and you are comfortable providing it.
- o You are probably going to have an emotional reaction. *That's okay.* Do what you can to regulate your reaction.
- o If needed, or possible, leave the situation/space where the mistake happened. Get some distance both physically and emotionally.
- o Get support from someone else, not the person you made the mistake with.
- o Work on processing your own thoughts and feelings. Avoid assuming the other person is wrong about what happened.
- o Understand your intent is not connected to their impact. You made a mistake, and they are reacting to that mistake.

Afterwards, once both of you have had some time to process your feelings, see what you can do to manage what happened. Wait until the other person is ready to communicate. This could be minutes, hours, days, or longer. The absolute best thing you can do for them and yourself in this situation is: be patient, and allow them to come to you. Trying to seek communication or contact with them may have a *severely* negative effect, possibly compounding the impact of the initial mistake in a traumatic way. Once they're ready, try some of the following:

- o Actively listen to what they have to say. Take notes, if needed.
- o When they're finished, validate their feelings, acknowledge you made a mistake, and state the mistake you made.
- o Apologize *unreservedly* for the harm you caused. (*Unreservedly*, in this context, means that you don't qualify your apology with excuses or victim-blaming, like, "How was I supposed to know?" or, "You never told me!") You can state *once* that you didn't mean to harm them—that the impact was unintentional. If you do this, make sure to add that you understand your lack of intent doesn't diminish the impact on them.
- o Ask what you can do to help resolve the situation, and listen actively to the answer.
- o If you are able, do what is needed. If you are not able, state clearly that you're not, why, and what you are willing/able to do instead.
- o If the other person states they are not willing to forgive, negotiate, or process what happened, accept that and move on.
- o Get outside-support to manage your feelings around what happened. (Don't make the all-too-common mistake of thinking that it will be easier to talk to the person involved in the situation, since they already know what happened, and you won't have to explain the circumstances again. This could lead to further harm.)
- o If the other person is not willing or able to communicate with you, get additional support to manage your own feelings around what happened without the aid of a resolution conversation.

If you find that mistakes are happening around you repeatedly, whether you are the person making the mistake or the person they are happening to, then it is time to reevaluate the situations you are in and your capacity. It may be that you need more information or education to stop the mistakes. It may be that you are subconsciously acting out old patterns, and need help to process and stop those patterns. It may be that you are with someone who is unhealthy for you, and you need to stop being around them.

Mistakes happen to all of us. We do them and they are done to us. It is a part of life, and we need to be able t recognize that, even when it involves consent. Unfortunately, there are times when Consent Violations are not mistakes.

Intentional Consent Violations

While most Consent Incidents are unintentional, caused by external impact, awareness issues, miscommunication, and other mistakes, some are done purposefully. These intentional Consent Incidents frequently lead to Consent Violations and harm for one or more people. If you have been involved in a Consent Violation, this may be a hard section to read. It was a hard section for us to write. Remember to take your time and get support when needed.

There are a wide range of behaviors that may lead to intentional Consent Violations. Here are some examples:

Overriding Requests: ignoring requests made by others, or answering requests with some version of, "Ye but I want to do this other thing instead." This type of behavior often starts out minor, and leads to increasing control of the situation by one of the people involved. It ignores the desires and autonomy of the other person/people.

Boundary Pushing: consistently pushing against boundaries set by others, usually to find a way around them. This often looks like arguing about the validity of the boundary, diminishing the importance of it, repeatedly reasserting how much desire there is for the thing in question, and/or simply ignoring the boundary until the other person says something. This ignores the autonomy of the other person, and often progresses to boundary crossing.

Boundary Crossing: ignoring or intentionally violating boundaries set by others. This behavior ignores a stated no, and simply continues the action or behavior that is being questioned. Such behavior often comes with strong defensiveness when it is called out, and may even include blaming the person who calls it out. It is significantly harmful.

Normalization: declaring a hurtful or harmful activity "normal" and/or saying "everybody does this" as a reason to ignore a boundary and/or intimidate a person into changing their boundary.

Shaming: telling someone their boundary exists because they are weak, insecure, stupid, not _____ enough, etc. Intentionally causing another person to think of themselves as wrong or bad in some way for attempting to set or hold reasonable boundaries.

Ignoring: intentionally forgetting or refusing to acknowledge boundaries during discussion, planning, or negotiation; avoiding or neglecting safety, consent, and aftercare agreements.

Manipulation and Coercion: attempting to change someone's level of agreement or boundaries through more subtle tactics. This type of behavior can look like arguing, reasonable debate, unrealistic expectations, or implied threat. Whatever the specific behavior involved, it is an attempt to convince, persuade, or turn a decisio into something the other person wants, without regard for autonomy and authenticity.

Controlling Behaviors: forcing one person to do what another wants through controlling environment and interactions. This can include controlling access to money, friends, family, self-care, emotional stability, independence, transportation, etc. These behaviors create a situation of dependence and doubt, first reducing and then destroying a person's autonomy. The person doing this will often blame the other, or attribute it to concern for them. Neither is true.

Direct Violence: forcing one person to do what another wants through the direct application of mental, emotional, physical, and/or sexual violence. This can include verbal or physical violence directed at a person or at the environment the person is in. It is always harmful, ignores the very concept of autonomy, and destroys a person's ability to consent. It often causes lasting harm and trauma, especially when done repeatedly.

This is not a complete list, but it gives an idea of the types of behavior that go along with intentional Consent Violations. You might notice these are similar to behaviors involved in cycles of abuse, domestic violence, and sexual harassment. That is because all of these involve the intentional violation of another person's consent and autonomy.

It's important to note several complexities. All of these fall along scales of severity and frequency. All of them happen to and are perpetrated by people of all identities. The vast majority of people have engaged in one or more of these behaviors at some point in their lives. And, it is the people who engage in one or more of them regularly who create the most harm, and are in need of intensive therapy, education, and behavioral change.

Take a breath. Pause. Take another one. This information can be difficult to process and take in. It can be uncomfortable, sad, angering, hurtful, or upsetting. And that's true when you're just reading about it. Encountering it directly can be overwhelming, at best.

We have one more concept to talk about before we move on to what you can do to make things better.

We talked about behaviors that often lead to Consent Violations. Because these are different from mistakes and other unintentional Consent Incidents, it's important to talk about another difference. Intentional behavior is more complicated than a person choosing a behavior. Intentional Consent Incidents can fall into two primary categories.

Emotionally Driven Intentional Incidents: These are situations where a person, due to a strong emotional reaction, violates someone's consent. This can happen through any of the above behaviors, and is harmful to the person subjected to it. It is also harmful to the person who does it.

These situations are complicated for many reasons. Often the person who violates consent like this does not feel or think they are doing it intentionally. They often feel like they are being driven by some internal force. There is intention, but it is an emotionally driven intention rather than a thought out or planned one.

There are a wide variety of reasons people find themselves in this place. People who perpetrate emotionally driven, intentional Consent Incidents are often acting out some emotional need, mistaken belief, strong social pressure, intense self-esteem issues, and/or their own trauma and abuse cycle. The person, for whatever reason, is unable to regulate their emotional state enough to prevent it from creating maladaptive behavior.

One of the most common examples comes out of intense emotional need. One person sees another, experiences a strong emotional desire for them, and rushes to act out that desire without stopping to see if the behavior is okay or wanted. This might be a person who rushes over to hug a friend they haven't seen in months. This can also be a person who, overcome with anger, lashes out and hits someone.

Another common example comes out of a sense of entitlement. This is where one person wants something from another, and believes they have the right to have it, regardless of the other person's boundaries or consent.

This could be a boss that demands extra work or favors from an employee. This can also be a person who grabs the genitals of another without asking. Most issues of entitlement come with some form of power differential.

There are many other possible examples. It is likely you have experienced something like this in your life. The primary feature is the inability to regulate behavior in response to an emotional reaction. In essence, this is a person acting out of need, without thinking about the impact on the other person.

The emotional nature of the act doesn't change the harm done—it doesn't change the fact that a Consent Violation happened. It does change how it can be handled. People who do this need to engage in significant behavioral change, and often some form of external intervention. For most, this change is possible, but only when the person is able to see the Consent Violation as wrong and/or harmful, and is willing to do the work to change.

The change can take some time. Depending on the severity of the emotional dysregulation, dysfunctional belief patterns, social pressure, self-esteem issues, and/or trauma, this type of work can take months, years, or even decades. During that time, it is important that the person has support—emotional, social, and professional—in order to promote the change to healthier behavior.

Intentional or Planned Incidents: These are situations where a person, knowingly and with forethought, intentionally violates the consent of another. This can be through any of the behaviors mentioned above. While these are the most rare forms of Consent Violations, they also tend to be the most damaging.

This is what most people think of when they hear the phrases Consent Incident or Consent Violation. While the vast majority of Consent Incidents are caused by environmental factors, miscommunications, mistakes, or emotionally driven behavior, it is the incidents perpetrated by intentional thought that get the most focus. They tend to cause the most intense damage, and are often repeated.

These situations are more direct. One person is choosing to violate the consent of another. This causes harm, violates autonomy, and should stop. That doesn't mean it is uncomplicated.

People engage in this behavior for a variety of reasons. For some, it is due to significant errors in belief, either about themselves or others. For some, there are culture, community, religious, or family beliefs that cause or enhance the problematic behavior. There could be mental and emotional health issues in play. There might be trauma or an abuse history being acted out.

None of these reasons excuse or diminish the behavior, they only provide context and directions for how to respond. Change has to start with recognition of the behavior, and the harm done to others. Remember, we are talking about changing the behavior, not the person.

If the person does want to change the behavior, and recognizes the harm caused to others and themselves, it can be a long process, depending on severity, length of time, and age. This often involves intense social, emotional, and mental work, ideally with the assistance of a professional coach, therapist, or support group. Having all three can help the most. The person needs to be able to both stop the harmful behavior, and learn new ways of interacting with others.

There are some who are either unable or unwilling to change their behavior. When this is the case, there are few options. The primary choice is to separate the person from the community they are harming. Where this crosses into legal territory, it means arrest. Where it stays in social territory, it means removal or shunning.

This may sound severe. Remember we are talking about intentional harm to another person. This category describes Consent Violations done with the knowledge that harm—sometimes intense and lasting harm—will be done to another human being.

Intentional Consent Incidents are thankfully not the majority of incidents, but they do need to be talked about and dealt with when they happen. People who engage in intentionally damaging behavior, either emotionally driven or planned, often start small and work up to greater harm. Too often they are not confronted or called on the early or small behaviors.

Our goal is a world where consent is the norm: where the vast majority of people act in a consensual manner with one another. The only way to get there is to catch poor consent behavior early, and work to re-educate people towards healthier and more adaptive behavior. This not only reduces the harm done, it creates a more aware community.

Start by recognizing these types of behavior and saying something when you see them. Let people know it is not okay to ignore someone's autonomy or cause them harm because they want something different. Tell everyone your consent is important. Tell them their consent is important.

Together, with work, things will change.

How do You Know if Someone's Consent has been Violated?

You might be wondering how you know if consent has been violated. We are often asked this question. It has both a simple and complicated answer.

Remember that all problematic consent interactions start with a Consent Incident. Something has happened involving consent. Then, after gathering information, talking with the people involved, and understanding the situation better, a determination can be made if consent was violated or broken.

As noted above, that determination can only be made by the person to whom it happened. This is the simple part. The person who has been impacted gets to decide if their consent was violated.

The violation can come due to circumstance, an unintentional mistake, emotionally driven behavior, or intentional behavior. Whether intentional or not is unimportant to whether it is a violation, only to how that violation is dealt with.

This means the person impacted doesn't get to determine if the violation was intentional or not. Only the person who engaged in the behavior can give context to its intention and driving force. It also means the person impacted rarely gets to decide what should happen to the person who did the action socially or legally.

They can, and should, set boundaries around communication and interaction for their own safety and wellbeing. They can, and should, seek support for their physical, emotional, and social well-being. But for someone who has been impacted by a Consent Violation, they should avoid trying to directly enforce behavioral change on the person who hurt them. To create social or legal impact, they need to appeal to people or organizations who have the power and ability to enforce behavioral change, ideally with understanding and compassion.

There are reasons why appealing to others is necessary. One, an individual rarely has the power to enforce behavioral change. This takes the greater influence and agency found in a collective or organization. Two, it's not fair to ask the person impacted to gather information. Rarely is it a good idea for a person who feels violated to talk to the person who violated them. Three, it's not fair to place the emotional burden of finding resources and enforcing change on someone who is working to deal with being violated.

For further complication, coming forward to ask for help is difficult. Many people have been ignored in the past when they try to talk about how they have been impacted. When not ignored, they are often ridiculed by their community for coming forward at all. Even when listened to, the necessity of retelling their story often causes additional trauma and pain.

It is important for Consent Incidents to be looked at, reviewed, and appropriately dealt with. It is important that people whose consent has been violated are given appropriate support, space for healing, and tools to help them grow and recover. It is important that people who have broken, violated, or damaged the consent of another are given appropriate support, education, space to change, tools to help them grow, and sufficient oversight.

All of these things takes time, resources, and organizational will.

There are no simple answers here. We are in an incredible time of change and growth around the concept of consent. There are new ideas being developed, tried, revised, and retired all the time. What follows are some things you can do.

What to do if You Violate Someone's Consent

As we talked about before, you will violate someone's consent. In fact, you have already. This doesn't make you a bad person. Remember, most Consent Incidents are unintentional. And, you still need to deal with it.

The most important thing you can do is recognize what has happened and your part in it. Avoid getting defensive or engaging in denial. Understand that someone has been hurt, you caused that hurt, and you need to do your best to repair it.

The basic steps are these:

1. Own the mistake
   - State, either out loud or in writing, exactly what happened.
   - Make it known that you are aware you messed up.
   - State your willingness to hear about their experience.

2. Honestly apologize
   - Express remorse for having caused them pain or distress.
   - Avoid questioning the person's experience.
   - Inform them that, regardless of your intentions, you recognize that you caused harm.

3. Make amends and attempt repair
   - Ask the other person what you can do to make things better.
     - It may be to stay away for a while. It may be to engage in regular conversations about how to move forward. It may be something else.
   - Stay present and listen to what they are saying. Avoid interrupting or offering suggestions unless asked.
   - If you can do what is requested, do it. If you can't, explain that you can't and ask to negotiate.

4. Update your consent framework
   - Reflect on the experience, and update how you view consent with this person.
   - Reflect on which of the basic consent concepts (capacity, informed consent, agreement/boundaries, and autonomy), were not upheld in this situation.
   - Ask yourself, "What blind spots came up? Were any new blind spots created? What can I do be more aware in the future?"

5. Strive to do better
    o Use your reflections to make the necessary changes.
    o Pay more attention to people's responses to your requests.
    o Seek out the information you need to understand yourself and others better.
    o Consider this an opportunity to improve yourself. Recovering from a Consent Incident is not just about repairing connection. It is about making sure you avoid the same behavior in the future.

Here are some specific things you can do if A) someone tells you that you have violated or broken their consent, or B) you recognize it yourself:

1. Take a deep breath. This is a hard and emotional thing to have happen. It can bring up a lot of different feelings.
    o Common feelings are anger, fear, sadness, guilt, shame, and anxiety. It can also remind you of old memories or traumas.
    o People often feel confused and uncertain at first.
    o Through the whole process, always remember to breathe.
2. Get support. Avoid thinking you need to go through this alone.
    o Find a friend or someone you trust to talk to about what happened.
    o Seek support from a therapist, counselor, or other professional who can help you process.
    o Engage people to help make day-to-day things easier while you're working through what happened.
3. Avoid reacting from an emotional or defensive place.
    o Take time to process your own thoughts and feelings before responding to the person who was impacted.
    o Make sure you can respond from a clearer and more thoughtful place.
    o Also understand that the longer you wait to respond, the larger the impact is likely to be on the other person.
4. Remember that intent does not equal impact. Your perception of what happened and what you meant in your actions or behavior, doesn't change how the other person experienced the event.
    o Avoid *arguing* that your intent was good, or that you didn't mean to hurt the other person. It will only make the other person feel unheard or dismissed.
5. If you do decide to communicate with the other person (and you can decide not to), keep your response clear, simple, and short.
    o If you are responding in writing, have someone else read over that response before you send it.
    o If you can, write your response, get a decent night's sleep, and read it over again before sending it.
6. Any response should include the following:
    o An acknowledgement of what happened, and what the other person tells you happened for them. If they tell you they were hurt, see that they are hurt, and tell them you see that. If they tell you their consent was violated, see that as true and acknowledge it.
    o A statement that you feel remorse about what happened, and are sorry for the hurt you caused.

- A request asking what they need in the moment, and what you can do to make amends.
- An acknowledgement that you have responsibility for your behavior. This can be a simple statement of acknowledgement, or a more inclusive statement of what behaviors you're going to do to take responsibility.
  - Remember, you have responsibility for your behavior if the other person was hurt, even if you did everything right. It doesn't make you a bad person. It just means you have a responsibility to do something about it.
- Avoid arguing or trying to emphasize your perspective. Stick to validation (Ex: "Your experiences and feelings are understandable and reasonable in the circumstances...) and acknowledgement (Ex: "I see the actions I did that lead us to this place...).

7. If what happened has been reported to a venue or organization, contact the organization and ask what their policy is for dealing with a Consent Incident.
   - If they have one, follow it and work with the organization to help create resolution.
   - Use the resources they provide to help reduce tension and emotional interactions.

8. Find resources to help you understand what happened and what you can do to help prevent it from happening again.
   - Take charge of getting more or better education. Look for resources to help you with understanding and behavioral change.
   - Consider enlisting someone to help you stay accountable to the mistake you made. This is someone you trust, but who will also call you on problematic behavior and help you talk out what to do about it.
   - For more significant mistakes, or if you're someone in a position of power/authority, consider forming an accountability circle. This is a group of people who can help: 1) call out problematic behavior, 2) process what happened and why, and 3) hold you accountable for future behavior.
   - Consider enlisting professional support from consent advocates, consultants, coaches, or therapists.

9. If you decide you want to post your experience online, remember some people will be supportive and others will be critical.
   - Make a conscious choice to step into the public space, and get additional support to help when things get tough.
   - Get someone to help you review and edit your posts before you put them up.
   - Do not post details about the other person without their explicit consent.

10. Remember dealing with a Consent Incident is a process—sometimes a long and emotional one. Take care of yourself, use your support network, and be gentle with yourself while you're going through it.

What to do if Your Consent has been Violated

Having your consent violated is a difficult and emotional thing. It can have a significant impact and bring up many different emotions and physical reactions. If this has happened to you, it is not easy. You are not alone. It an experience shared by many.

Remember, you get to decide what has happened to you and its impact. A lot of people are going to have opinions and ideas, but you get to come to your own decisions around this complicated topic. You have the right to make decisions about what is right for you.

Here are some ideas that may help:

1. Take a deep breath. This is a hard and emotional thing. It can bring up a lot of different feelings.

   o Common feelings are anger, fear, sadness, guilt, shame, and anxiety. It can also invoke old memories or traumas.

   o People often feel confused and uncertain at first.

   o Through the whole process, always remember to breathe.

2. Get support. Avoid thinking you need to go through this alone.

   o Find a friend or someone you trust to talk to about what happened.

   o Seek support from a therapist, counselor, or other professional who can help you process.

   o Engage people to help make day-to-day things easier while you're working through what happened.

3. Take the time you need. Some people process things quickly. Other people need time to work through things.

   o There's no right or wrong answer to how much time you "should" take to process. It's different for everyone.

4. Think about what you want or need. Everyone is going to have an opinion on what you "should" do.

   o Use the time to think about what you want, what's right for you, and what you want your boundaries to be.

   o You have every right to make these decisions for yourself and to request that the people around you respect your decisions.

   o If you need help, engage your support network.

5. If you decide you want to tell the person who broke your consent, make sure you have other support in place. Understand that they will have emotional reactions too, may see the event differently, and may not be able to give you the response you need.

   o *Make sure you are telling them for yourself, to help you heal or process, and not out of a need for a specific response. Setting up expectations for a particular response is likely to result in disappointment if they respond differently, and may even cause you more harm. Running through many scenarios in your mind for how they might respond may help prepare you for a variety of outcomes, but try not to become attached to any particular one.*

   o If you reach out, keep your messages short, to the point, and as calm as possible.

   o Tell them what happened and how it impacted you. Avoid blaming language. (Ex: "It was your fault..." or, "Why were you being so spiteful/hurtful/mean?") Talk about your experience and your feelings. (Ex: "When you said/did (direct quote or action), I felt (feeling at the time, avoiding the use of the phrase 'I felt like...')")

   o Use behavioral language. Talk about the behaviors and how those behaviors impacted you. Be as specific as you can. It will help them to know as accurately as possible what words/actions/behaviors need to be addressed or changed.

- Tell them what you want from them and what they can do to make amends for what happened (That is, if you know. This can take time to figure out, and may—in part—depend on their response.)
- Give them time to respond. This may be a long process for them, and it's better for them to have time to give a thoughtful response, rather than a hasty or knee-jerk reaction.
- Remember that while you can decide impact, you cannot know intent. Avoid attributing intent to the behavior. (Ex: "I think you did it that way on purpose," or, "How could you do something like that?")
- Have someone else read over what you write or talk out what you are going to say before communicating.

6. If you decide you want to report what happened, which you have every right to do, contact the space, company, or venue where it happened (if there was one) and ask what their policy is for reporting a Consent Incident or Violation.
   - If they have one, do what you can to follow it. If they don't have one, ask them to work with someone who does.
   - If they have one, but it is either insufficient or they do not act on it, get support from other leaders in your community to help create more structure around intervention.
   - If you decide to contact the police to report the incident as a crime, get support from friends, advocates, and/or a lawyer to help you through the process.
   - Reporting can be a difficult and stressful thing, and there is often important timing connected to laws or policy enforcement. Be prepared (and/or get support) to respond to inquiries from the authorities within the timeline and parameters they ask for from you.

7. If you decide you want to post your experience online, that is your right too. Remember, while some people may be supportive, others will be critical.
   - Make a conscious choice to step into the public space, and make sure you have additional support to help when things get tough.
   - Get someone to help you review and edit your posts before you put them up. Consider locking the post to block all replies, or getting someone to review responses and filter out the non-constructive/non-supportive replies.

8. Remember, dealing with a Consent Incident is a process—sometimes a long and emotional one. Take care of yourself, use your support network, and be gentle with yourself while you're going through it.

What to do When You Read or Hear about a Consent Violation

You may hear about Consent Violations by reading about them on the internet, or hearing about them at your workplace, in your community, or in your social circle. This can be a difficult or upsetting experience. It may bring up emotions and physical sensations. You might identify with one (or all) of the people involved, or wonder about times in your life that were similar.

It can feel overwhelming. First, take a deep breath. Remember: this isn't happening to you, and you can stop engaging whenever you need.

Second, try to remember the complexity and nuance you have learned about in this book. These things are never simple, even if they appear that way at first. Most of what you read or hear will be coming from a single perspective.

Third, withhold any judgement, and wait to take action until you know more. If you want to do something, even if that is only deciding what you think happened, take the time and do the necessary work. If you never get more information, don't judge or take action.

Here are a few suggestions for when you encounter a Consent Incident or potential Consent Violation:

DO:	AVOID:
Recognize that any Consent Incident or Violation is complicated and can be placed on a broad spectrum.	**Engaging in black/white, either/or thinking around the topic.**
Offer support to the people involved. Dealing with a Consent Incident or Violation, especially when it is made public, is hard.	**Stating an opinion when you don't know all the details or facts.**
Recognize that only the person whose consent has been violated gets to determine if and how much that incident impacted them. It is also their right to decide how they want to deal with it.	**Defining how other people should feel or what their intent was in a given situation.**
Talk about issues of consent on your own feed/wall/blog/etc. These are important things to talk about and share ideas on.	**Engaging in debate about an idea in a place where someone is talking about their personal experience, seeking support, or asking for help.**
Ask yourself before making a public statement whether or not someone will be harmed, or if the risk of harm will be increased. Remember, real people are on the other side of the comments you're making.	**Shaming or threatening people because you disagree with them.**
Encourage people to seek support, get help, and better educate themselves about consent.	**Criticizing anyone for wanting to learn, grow, or change.**

Recognize that if we want people to come forward, either as someone who has had their consent violated or as someone who violated another's consent, we need to support them—, both emotionally and logistically— in doing so. Help create structures where everyone they can get emotional support, education, and good consultation.	**Thinking this process is simple or easy.**
Encourage organizations you work with to develop, use, and improve consent policies and procedures.	**Ignoring this critically important issue**

Chapter 9: Next Steps

There are so many things we wanted to talk about in this book, and even now, at the end, we've only scratched the surface. But that's where a primer starts: with basic concepts and ideas.

We started with what consent is, and talked about capacity, information, agreement, and autonomy. We looked at consent as part of many different kinds of relationships, and also how it relates to sex. We talked about the complexity of consent when it goes wrong.

Be honest: Do you feel like you know more or less about consent now than when you started?

For many at this stage, the answer is both. You have learned a lot. We packed as much into this first book as we could. At the same time, you have learned there is much more to consent than first meets the eye.

We know this book hasn't covered everything. In the interest of keeping things simple and accessible in this initial overview, we opted not to delve into deeper topics like the intersections of consent and racism, sexism, and privilege. We haven't looked at the significant impact of trauma, trauma response, and shame, on consent and consensual interactions. We've only scratched the surface on the complex issues of autonomy, identity, and how to manage Consent Incidents. There is a lot more to talk about.

Our goal was to create a foundation for how to think about this complex topic. Much like primers of old, we have worked to give you the basics. These will help inform your thoughts on consent and its role in your life. We hope you will take this information and integrate it with other knowledge and ideas you already have, and maybe even those you may have in the future.

We are going to continue to write about more aspects of consent. We're hoping to cover topics like "how to work with consent as a leader," and "how to manage accountability programs." While we work on those, the Consent Academy will also continue to produce workshops and trainings, to meet as many kinds of educational needs and learning styles as we can, and reach as many with our message as is possible. There is so much more to learn and study.

And, learning isn't enough. As you read through these pages, you saw over and over again that *knowing* a thing isn't the same as *doing* it. To get better at consent, you will need to practice the communication and behaviors that go along with the knowledge. Here are some ways to practice:

o **Talk About Consent:** It may seem like a little thing, but it is important. Have conversations with the people in your life about the importance of consent, how you view it, and what your expectations are. Talk about consent when it comes up in the media or in your personal life. Talk about how to manage Consent Incidents, and what can be done to make things better.

o **Use Consent:** Don't just talk about it. Use what you've learned to make requests of others, and to honor their consent when they give or withhold it. See other people as worthy of consensual interactions, and practice with them. Ask before you touch someone. Ask before using someone else's things. Ask people what they want, and confine your behavior to what they tell you. Wait until you get an explicit and/or enthusiastic *yes*. Stop when someone says *no*.

- **Focus on Autonomy in Your Interactions:** Autonomy is the cornerstone of consent. Recognize the inherent right of the people around you to make choices about their own body, mind, emotions, and spirit. It will change the way you look at interactions with them. Recognizing that you have the same inherent right can change the way you look at people's interactions with you. With practice, it can give you more confidence in making decisions centered in your own needs, and in calling people on their lack of respect.

- **Remind Others to Use Consent with You:** Let other people know you expect them to act in a consensual way. Remind them when they forget. Set boundaries and hold them, even when it's uncomfortable. When your consent is broken or violated, ask the other person to make amends.

- **Build Consent Practices:** Practice with people you trust to get comfortable both giving and receiving consent. Be awkward and make mistakes. Use consent to create better frameworks and more consent-based relationships, and to promote safety and more openings for greater connection and intimacy. It's a win/win.

- **Incorporate Consent into Your Sex Life and Sexuality:** Use what you have learned to have more consensual interactions around sex. Practice being consensual in all of your sexual interactions, even with long-term partners. Use consent to create more authentic interactions, greater intimacy, and more space for pleasure.

- **When Consent Goes Wrong, Do Better:** You will be involved in a Consent Incident. Sometimes your consent will be broken or violated. Sometimes you will be the one doing the breaking. Use your knowledge and understanding to practice better self-care, responses, and understanding. Acknowledge your responsibility and work towards healing.

- **Practice, Practice, Practice:** Use consent in big ways, small ways, and every way in-between. Use it when you feel comfortable and when you feel uncertain. Use it when it's easy, and especially when it's hard. Consent is a skill and the only way to get better at it is to practice. With time and effort, you will get better.

Consent may not be simple. It may be confusing, difficult, or even daunting. Stick with it and keep trying, because there will also be times when having consent feels amazing.

There will be times when being with someone who truly wants to be with you will feel like the best thing in the world. There will be times when knowing—and being able to communicate—what you want will feel empowering. And there will be times when knowing you have the inherent right to give an honest answer, yes or no, will change the course of your life.

Consent has done all of these things for us. It has changed our lives and the lives of the people we love, work with, enjoy time with, and met for just a moment or two. It is that powerful, and that fundamental.

Our goal is to change the world, one consensual interaction at a time. With each new moment of consent—each time consent is affirmed and upheld—we build towards a new way of living. We build towards a culture where consent is the norm, and people treat each other with respect.

We hope you will join us in that world.

About the Authors: While the Consent Academy is an Education Collective, and all of our members contributed with ideas, concepts, and understanding, five of our members took that work and put words to pap to create this text.

Rachel Bowen (Upper Left) has a passion for helping people make breakthroughs and uncover their power. She has helped countles people transform their lives and find success and personal freedom. In addition to being a proud co-author of this book, she is an International Success Coach, Speaker, Accountability & Consent Consultant, Educator, and the Deputy Director of Consent Academy.

Leah Hirch (Lower Left): Leah is a lifelong consent enthusiast and advocate. Through her experiences in health care, the Consent Academy, and as Assistant to the Director of the Pan Eros Foundation, she continues to reach many who are eager to further their understanding of consent.

Lara-Ashley Monroe, MA (Upper Middle) is an advocate for healthy living through physical, mental and emotional awareness, and promotes strong relationships through respect and consent. She works as a management consultant, helping teams to recognize areas o lowered efficiency, improve processes, and encourage personal and team growth. Her enthusiasm for working in complex situations has led her to teaching consent and exploring innovative ways to approach this topic.

Sar Surmick, LMFT (Lower Right) founded the Consent Academy in 2016 to both promote consent and bring together amazing minds. Sar is a consent advocate, author, speaker, and international educator. In addition to being the director of the Consent Academy Sar has a private therapy practice in Redmond, WA, focusing on identity work, consensual non-monogamy, and alternative sexualities.

Kelley O'Hanlon, LMHC (Upper Right) has a private therapy practice in Redmond, WA, working with polyamorous, kinky, and gee folks of all persuasions and fandoms. She teaches consent to help clients explore and express autonomy and authenticity in all areas of their lives.

For more information on the Consent Academy and all the things we do to help people understand consent, please visit us:

www.consent.academy

Glossary of Terms

Agency: the ability to exert power or influence.

Autonomy: the ability to say what happens with and to your body, mind, and spirit; the freedom of choice for all of these parts of your "self" which are working in conjunction. This includes being able to choose how lon something happens, free from external control or influence. It is an inherent right of all people, regardless of their appearance, age, relationship status, social standing, or any other identity or factor.

Boundary: a stated limit that says what you're not willing to do or what behaviors you're not willing to engage in.

Boundary Crossing: ignoring or intentionally violating boundaries set by others. This behavior ignores a stated no, and simply continues the action or behavior that is being questioned. Such behavior often comes with strong defensiveness when it is called out, and may even include blaming the person who calls it out. It is significantly harmful.

Boundary Pushing: consistently pushing against boundaries set by others, usually to find a way around them. This often looks like arguing about the validity of the boundary, diminishing the importance of it, repeatedly reasserting how much desire there is for the thing in question, and/or simply ignoring the boundary until the other person says something. This ignores the autonomy of the other person, and often progresses to boundary crossing.

Capacity: the physical, mental, emotional, and social ability to A) give or receive an honest and voluntary agreement, or B) set or receive an honest boundary for a specific activity.

Coded Yes: a term or phrase that gives the sense of agreement without communicating a clear yes. It's a w for someone to agree without using the actual word, and is common when someone feels they shouldn't agree t something even when they want to. This is an attempt to give consent without being explicit.

Confirmation Bias: a bias where we are more likely to see/hear things that agree with what we want, an less likely to see/hear the things that don't agree.

Consent: a voluntary agreement, made without coercion, between persons with decision-making capacity, knowledge, understanding, and autonomy. The use of consent allows a person to affirm or deny any request or interaction.

Consent Incident: an event, involving consent, where something has gone wrong. In a Consent Incident, there is no assumption of intention, guilt, or fault. Just as there is no assumption of victim or perpetrator, there is no assumption of harm or trauma. This is an event that needs consideration, review, and outside support. When a Consent Incident occurs we want to understand what happened, and figure out what to do next.

Consent Violation: an event where a person believes their consent was broken, a set boundary was crossed, or lasting harm was caused during a Consent Incident. Only the person who experiences the event gets to decide if their consent was violated. There is no external assumption of intent, while still recognizing that harm has been caused. This means that everyone does their best to avoid assigning "blame" or "fault," and assumes that the person who did the actions that negatively affected someone else did not mean to cause harm with their actions. All parties involved deserve emotional support, social support, education, and sometimes intervention by an organization or team. When a Consent Violation occurs, the goal is to find ways of reducing the impact to the affected party, and preventing the harm from happening again.

Control Bias (or the Illusion of Control): a bias where we are more likely to believe we have greater control over a situation or external events than we do. This includes control over other people's desires and decisions.

Controlling Behaviors: forcing one person to do what another wants through controlling environment and interactions. This can include controlling access to money, friends, family, self-care, emotional stability, independence, transportation, etc. These behaviors create a situation of dependence and doubt, first reducing and then destroying a person's autonomy. The person doing this will often blame the other, or attribute it to concern for them. Neither is true.

Direct Violence: forcing one person to do what another wants through the direct application of mental, emotional, physical, and/or sexual violence. This can include verbal or physical violence directed at a person or at the environment the person is in. It is always harmful, ignores the very concept of autonomy, and destroys a person's ability to consent. It often causes lasting harm and trauma, especially when done repeatedly.

Emotional Perception Bias: a bias where we are more likely to see/hear emotions similar to what we're feeling, even when the other person isn't feeling that way. We are less likely to see/hear emotions that disagree or are opposed to what we're feeling.

Ignoring: intentionally forgetting or refusing to acknowledge boundaries during discussion, planning, or negotiation; avoiding or neglecting safety, consent, and aftercare agreements.

Informed Consent: all sides of an interaction have sufficient information, and understanding of that information, to be able to make an honest and clear decision about engaging in an interaction or not; knowing what is being requested and the boundaries around that request. Informed consent focuses on honest and open communication, and hinges on all parties having enough information to make a decision. Consent cannot exist where there is insufficient information, where there is inaccurate or dishonest information, or where any of the people involved are unable to understand the information.

Intent: the sum of our thoughts, feelings, desires, and beliefs that go into a decision to engage in a behavior. It can be either conscious or unconscious. Intent happens prior to an action, and may take minutes or fractions of a second to form. Once formed, intent is influenced by our physical, mental, and emotional capacities before it becomes a behavior. Intent is not the behavior that results: it is the driving force that causes a behavior.

Impact: the effect a behavior has. When a behavior is initiated by someone else, we perceive it, and then we have a response. Those thoughts and feelings are the impact. The response is influenced by our perception of the behavior, our current physical, mental, and emotional capacity, and our systems of belief and/or understanding. Impact is not the behavior it resulted from; impact is how the behavior lands within you. To put it another way, impact is not the actions done nor the words spoken by the other person; it is your reaction that arises in response to someone else's actions or words.

Manipulation and Coercion: attempting to change someone's level of agreement or boundaries through more subtle tactics. This type of behavior can look like arguing, reasonable debate, unrealistic expectations, or implied threat. Whatever the specific behavior involved, it is an attempt to convince, persuade, or turn a decision into something the other person wants, without regard for autonomy and authenticity.

Normalization: declaring a hurtful or harmful activity "normal" and/or saying "everybody does this" as a reason to ignore a boundary and/or intimidate a person into changing their boundary.

Overriding Requests: ignoring requests made by others, or answering requests with some version of, "Yes, but I want to do this other thing instead." This type of behavior often starts out minor, and leads to increasing control of the situation by one of the people involved. It ignores the desires and autonomy of the other person/people.

Perception Bias: a bias where we are more likely to see/hear things that match what we want, and less likely to see/hear the things that don't match.

Shaming: telling someone their boundary exists because they are weak, insecure, stupid, not _____ enough, etc. Intentionally causing another person to think of themselves as wrong or bad in some way for attempting to set or hold reasonable boundaries.

Superiority Bias: a bias where we tend to overestimate our own desirable qualities, and underestimate our undesirable qualities, relative to others.

Bibliography

Bilsky, L. (2009). " 'Speaking Through The Mask': Israeli Arabs and the Changing Faces of Israeli Citizenship, Middle East Law and Governance, 1, 2, 166-209.

Boyer, Edward J. and Garcia, Kenneth J. "Rock Hudson's Male Lover Is Awarded $14.5 Million." The Washington Post. February 16, 1989.

Cf. Haynes v. Washington, 373 U.S. 503, 512-513 (1963); Haley v. Ohio, 332 U.S. 596, 601 (1948) (opinion of MR. JUSTICE DOUGLAS).

College Sexual Assault, Anderson, Nick & Clement, Scott, The Washington Post, 6/12/2015 - https://www.washingtonpost.com/sf/local/2015/06/12/1-in-5-women-say-they-were-violated

Festinger, L. (1957). *A Theory of cognitive dissonance*. Stanford, CA: Stanford University Press.

Green, Douglas S T, and C Ronald MacKenzie. "Nuances of informed consent: the paradigm of regional anesthesia." HSS journal : the musculoskeletal journal of Hospital for Special Surgery vol. 3,1 (2007): 115-8. doi:10.1007/s11420-006-9035-y

Heshmat, Shahram (2015, April) What is Confirmation Bias? *Psychology Today*. Retrieved from: https://www.psychologytoday.com/us/blog/science-choice/201504/what-is-confirmation-bias

Johnson, Allan G. (2006) *Privilege, Power, and Difference 2nd Ed*. Boston, MA: McGraw-Hill

Kabat-Zinn, J. (2006) *Mindfulness for Beginners*. Boulder, CO: Sounds True, Inc

Kabat-Zinn, J. (2013) *Full Catastrophe Living (Revised Edition): Using the Wisdom of Your Body and Mind to Face Stress, Pain, and Illness*. New York, NY: Bantam Books

PPFA Consent Survey, Planned Parenthood, 2015 - www.plannedparenthood.org/files/1414/6117/4323/Consent_Survey.pdf

Schloendorff v the Society of the New York Hospital, 211 NY 125 105 NE 92 1914 LEXIS 1028 (1914).

Speelman, C. (2005). Skill acquisition: History, questions, and theories. In C. Speelman & K. Kinser (Eds.), Beyond the learning curve: The construction of mind (pp. 26-64). Oxford: Oxford University Press

Supreme Court Reporter, "Miranda v. State of Arizona (86 S.Ct. 1602)," June 13, 1966

The Power of No, Sills, Judith, *Psychology Today*, 11/05/2013 - https://www.psychologytoday.com/us/articles/201311/the-power-no

Made in the USA
San Bernardino, CA
11 February 2020